Walter W. Felts

The voter's handbook

natural law in the business world, showing that natural law should be the

model for institutions and laws of government

Walter W. Felts

The voter's handbook
natural law in the business world, showing that natural law should be the model for institutions and laws of government

ISBN/EAN: 9783337712037

Printed in Europe, USA, Canada, Australia, Japan

Cover: Foto ©Andreas Hilbeck / pixelio.de

More available books at **www.hansebooks.com**

THE VOTER'S HANDBOOK

NATURAL LAW IN THE BUSINESS WORLD

SHOWING THAT NATURAL LAW SHOULD BE THE MODEL FOR
INSTITUTIONS AND LAWS OF GOVERNMENT, FOR THE
GOVERNMENT OF NATIONAL AND INTERNATIONAL
COMMERCE, AND FOR THE DIRECTION OF
GENERAL BUSINESS AND TRADE

BY

WALTER W. FELTS

AUTHOR OF "PRINCIPLES OF SCIENCE" AND "THE CIRCULAR
SYSTEM OF SCIENCE"

PUBLISHED BY THE AUTHOR
112 FIFTH AVENUE, NEW YORK
1897

CONTENTS

	PAGE
PREFACE	7
INTRODUCTORY REMARKS	9
CIRCULATION	17
Circuit of Business—Circulation of Money	23
Government Ownership of Railroads, Telegraph, and Telephone	30
Municipal Ownership of Street-car Lines	32
Evil Effects of Trusts, Combines, etc.	34
"Value Received" a Law of Nature	37
Nature Denies Man the Right to Rule	40
TRUE RELATIONS OF LAND, LABOR, AND CAPITAL	42
The People—the Government	52
Politics Involves all Personal Interests	56
The Duty of the People	60
The People have the Right to Criticize Faithless Public Servants	71
BIMETALLISM	73
Natural Law and Bimetallism	74
Principle of Bimetallism in Nature	80
Natural Laws the True Model for Human Laws	85
Three Laws for Restraint of Greed	88
An Appeal for Patriotism	91
A Talk with Voters	94

	PAGE
Beware of Political Deceptions	100
Demoralizing Effects of Political Evils	102
First Seeds of Anarchy	107
FREE TRADE	109
Natural Law Enjoins Free Trade	117
The Brotherhood of Man	121
Restrict Immigration	122
GOD IN NATURE	125

PREFACE

THE belief that there is a large field of usefulness for such a book as I herewith present to all lovers of just laws and good government induced me to write this condensed treatise on "Natural Law in the Business World." If it be well received and there seem to be a demand for an enlarged edition, it will be forthcoming.

I present this advance edition with confidence that it will be read and appreciated by all right-thinking people. It will be as much to its credit to be denounced by some as to be commended by others. In this sense I can say with the poet Pope, "I write for such as it is a credit to please."

THE AUTHOR.

INTRODUCTORY REMARKS

He who argues most is least certain of truth in what he affirms or denies. He who is certain of the truth can present it without argument. On the other hand, error requires much argument in the endeavor to prove that it is not error. For this reason I abandoned skepticism long ago. I discovered that it consists altogether in argument, not to prove anything, but to disprove everything. I am no longer skeptical in anything. Until I am convinced I may be uncertain, but not skeptical. I hold judgment in abeyance for conclusive proof, and when the evidence is all in I then decide positively. If it be error I reject it, if truth I accept it, and there it ends.

My process of investigation is not argument. One is in no position to argue a matter or question which he has not investigated far enough to place himself beyond mere uncertainty.

In writing this little book I have nothing to argue. I have some great truths to present, and I present them in as clear and concise form as possible.

Touching political economy, I have read some, thought much, and felt, heard, and seen much more.

For years I have lived so close to nature's heart that I could feel the warmth of her love and hear her rapturous songs of truth. She bade me look, and I have seen beyond and within her outward forms and beheld the unseen reality of her being. If man may be wise, powerful, just, a mathematician, an astronomer, a chemist, a geologist, and even a statesman, then nature is wisdom, power, justice, mathematics, astronomy, chemistry, geology, and true statesmanship.

Error is nowhere to be found but in man, and this is because he abuses his free agency and would be wiser than nature. In his egotism and selfishness he formulates fine-spun theories and founds institutions best adapted to the gratification of his lusts. He prefers to live far away from nature because he loves error—"loves darkness rather than light, because his deeds are evil." Man sacrifices everything to present gratification. Nature beckons to him, and he turns his face toward inviting error. She pleads with him, and he hearkens to seducing error. She afflicts him with the penalties of her laws, and he embraces error the more fondly.

The whole difficulty lies in man's desire to free himself from restraints that exact moral purity. That is the logic of skepticism. For every well-authenticated truth man substantiates he invents a thousand groundless theories. More effort has been put forth to patch up errors so as to counterfeit a single truth than, if rightly directed, would discover a thousand genuine truths. Malthus introduced the theory of "the survival of the fittest" in that he claimed that population tends to crowd upon subsistence, and the transparent assumption became a cardinal principle of political economy. As if to scientifically demonstrate that theory, Darwin, Huxley, Spencer, and other authorities of our modern school of scientists formulated a theory of evolution which accounts for the origin of man by bald assumptions and a process of reasoning which, if possible, would give character to sophistry.

These theories are but the logical and philosophical outgrowth of materialism, and materialism is the legitimate offspring of egotism and selfishness. The unbridled freedom of egotism and selfishness naturally rebels against the restraints of moral purity. To justify the breaking away of these restraints, it is necessary to prove that the restraints do not exist in fact. And so an unbroken line of theories is formulated having in view that end. To prove that this assertion is true, I have only to remind the reader that science is dominated by skepticism. The proudest achievement of accepted science to-day, as regarded by the world, is not so much what it is able to prove as what it is supposed to be able to disprove.

Let it be understood that I am not attacking the great truths of science that have passed beyond the province of discussion. I have reference only to theories that have sprung from the one great theory of materialism. These theories, like a poisonous vine, have wound themselves about the tree of science so skilfully that in many places it is difficult to distinguish the tree and its branches from the vine and its luxuriant foliage of sophistry. And these theories have done and are doing the world incalculable harm. In all their tendencies they are debasing; they tend to cast men downward rather than to lift them upward. Indeed, they are in a large degree primarily responsible for all false theories of human government. Looked upon as the embodiment of true science, and coming with the authority and force of their recognized leaders, these theories present themselves in evidence that nature is animated by blind fatalism and that man is a sort of accidental product of the evolutions of accident. This renders nature purposeless and man bound by no restraints other than those which he himself may authorize and enforce. How debasing the belief in such theories!

And if the mere belief in erroneous theories plays havoc with the moral constitution of men, how much more can unjust and inhuman institutions and laws of government under which men must live undermine manhood, dethrone every ideal of purity, and break down all the restraints of lawlessness!

This nation, aye, this civilization, is drifting rapidly toward that point. It is my belief that there is a sufficient number of men, however, who, when they know the right and dare to do it, will turn back the tide of error upon itself, and roll away the great stone of oppression from the sepulcher of human liberty, that she may come forth, resurrected to newness of life.

If this little book will start a ripple of popular sentiment in the great current events that will join with the tidal wave of peaceful revolution setting in from the West and South, I shall feel that I have not lived in vain, even if I should never accomplish more. WALTER W. FELTS.

NEW YORK CITY, December 7, 1896.

God give us men! A time like this demands
Strong minds, great hearts, true faith, and ready hands;
Men whom the lust of office does not kill;
Men whom the spoils of office cannot buy;
Men who possess opinions and a will;
Men who have honor; men who will not lie;
Men who can stand before a demagogue
And damn his treacherous flatteries without winking;
Tall men, sun-crowned, who live above the fog
In public duty and in private thinking.
For while the rabble with their thumb-worn creeds,
Their large profession and their little deeds,
Mingle in selfish strife, lo! Freedom weeps,
Wrong rules the land, and waiting Justice sleeps.
Dr. J. G. Holland.

CIRCULATION

As a term to express a principle in nature, there is no word of deeper and broader meaning. I need not define the word "circulation." We all know what it means in a general way, as, for instance, in its application to the air, the blood, etc. We all know that animal life is dependent on the circulation of the blood, and that the air purifies itself by circulation; we know that water becomes stagnant when it ceases to circulate. But if we look deeper into this subject we shall see that all nature is dependent upon the active principle of circulation. Science teaches us that there is no such condition as rest; that there is nothing in all the universe that is fixed or stationary; it teaches that all things are in perpetual motion or circulation. The grandest operation of the principle of circulation is the revolution of planets around the sun, and the revolution of suns around other larger central suns. So far as the astronomer knows, the circulation of the heavenly bodies is infinite in space and endless in duration.

The revolutions of the earth on its axis and around the sun give us the perpetual round of day and night and the seasons. The round of time wrings all the changes in nature which come and go in the round of birth, growth, death, and decay, corresponding to spring, summer, autumn, and winter. These are the four annual heart-beats of nature that send the vitalizing and death-giving agencies through all her arteries of circulation. Out of her dust spring the vegetable and animal kingdoms, which grow, mature, decline, then decay and return to dust. The renewal and reproduction of animal and vegetable life is a cyclic action through series of changes from seed to seed. Between the vegetable and animal are reciprocal and dependent actions, which form a circuit of vitalizing agencies. The wants of one are supplied by the wastes of the other, the sustenance of both being mutually dependent upon rounds of reciprocal actions. The close connections and relations of the vegetable and animal kingdoms form a most complete circuit of life-giving agencies.

In all nature about us we see the operation of the principle of circulation. Moisture is raised from the earth by the heat of the sun, and again falls in rain, snow, hail, and dew. There is a perpetual round of evaporation and precipitation of moisture.

And then we note the circulation of the waters of the earth; the rivers and streams, fed by falling snows and rains, pouring into oceans, seas, and lakes water that is perpetually drawn from the earth by evaporation. The ocean currents perpetually circulate from the polar regions toward the equator, and from the equator toward the poles. The polar ice-

EXPLANATION OF FIG. 1.

The annexed cut (Fig. 1) is from an original drawing, and illustrates the underlying principle of circulation. The outer circle shows the position of the earth every twenty-four hours in its orbit around the sun. The seasons—spring, summer, autumn, and winter—are marked by the accompanying round of change—birth, growth, death, and decay. This is the great circuit of change around which swing in ceaseless tide all the developments of birth, growth, death, and decay in nature. Under this great law all the elements and developments of activities in nature have their circuits and circulation, some of which are described in the accompanying reading matter.

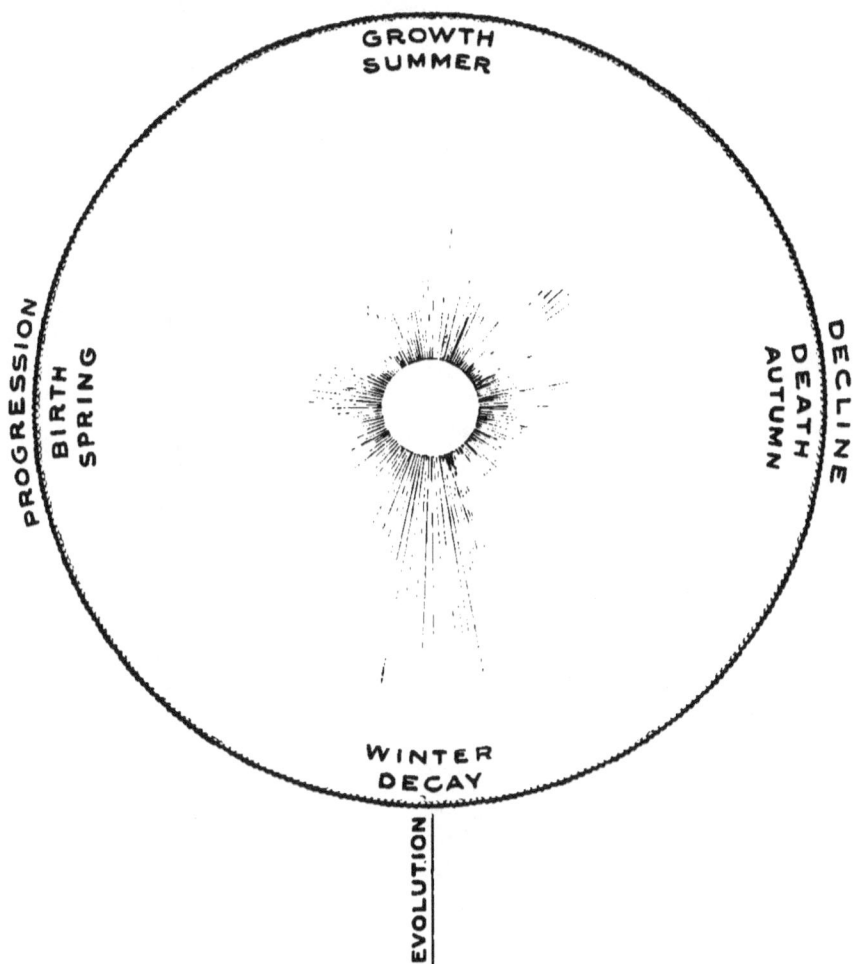

EXPLANATION OF FIG. 1.

The annexed cut (Fig. 1) is from an original drawing, and illustrates the underlying principle of circulation. The outer circle shows the position of the earth every twenty-four hours in its orbit around the sun. The seasons—spring, summer, autumn, and winter—are marked by the accompanying round of change—birth, growth, death, and decay. This is the great circuit of change around which swing in ceaseless tide all the developments of birth, growth, death, and decay in nature. Under this great law all the elements and developments of activities in nature have their circuits and circulation, some of which are described in the accompanying reading matter.

fields are broken up by the flow of the warm waters of the equator, and the ice-drifts are borne away by the polar stream to be melted by the warm ocean waters of the equatorial belt.

The winds and breezes indicate the circulation of the air. These, with ocean streams and the tides which periodically circulate the oceans of the globe, keep the waters of the ocean from becoming stagnant and much of its surface from becoming matted by vegetable growth.

And then, in the animal kingdom we note the circulation of the blood. Animal life depends upon it just as vegetable life depends upon the circulation of sap. All animate nature depends upon the circulation of blood and of sap for existence. This is the animating, the life-giving principle of all animate nature.

Now man, with all he is and has, is but a part of the vast machinery of nature. Man cannot violate the laws of nature with impunity. Nature inflicts punishment on all alike for violations of her laws. These laws of nature are supreme over all, and operative from the minutest detail even to all the conditions of the highest civilization attainable. Nature's laws are fixed principles and self-operative. They govern mind as well as matter, morals as well as mechanics.

There is no escaping or evading the operations of natural laws. They may be slow in their operations, but they are mathematically sure. The rich and powerful among men may ignore or even defy natural law in their imaginary greatness, but they will find, even as Solomon found, at the end of all the vain pomp and glory, nothing but "vanity and vexation of spirit."

An association of millionaires into a powerful combine for the purpose of absorbing the wealth of the land may fancy that they can override the laws of finance, which are governed by natural law, but they will find, as did Samson, that they cannot escape the crash of the temple of state which their greed is crowding down upon their own heads.

And this brings us directly to the subject under discussion—financial circulation. It is the banding together of millionaires into powerful associations for the purpose of absorbing the wealth of the country that violates the natural law of financial circulation. So long as money is the legal standard of values, so long will its free circulation be absolutely essential to general prosperity.

While the free coinage of silver would temporarily vitalize our industries and greatly stimulate trade, yet, with the unrestricted operation of powerful corporations and trusts, the arteries of financial circulation, which are already tapped, would be kept open, from which would continue to flow the life-blood of national prosperity. This nation—and, indeed, many more—needs free financial circulation much more than free coinage of silver.

To make it clear that our present financial system of circulation violates the natural law of circulation, let us suppose that the law of the circulation of moisture were violated,—that much of the moisture thrown off by evaporation were in some way absorbed,—what would be the effect on vegetable and animal life? Drought to the extent of the absorption of moisture would follow. There would be little rain or snow, and vegetation would be too meager to sustain life of animal or man.

Suppose the circulation of the air were suspended; how long would any climate remain healthful? Very soon the air would become stagnant and foul, followed by the ravages of disease.

Suppose the free circulation of the blood were interrupted by excessive bleeding or by bandaging the limbs and forcing the blood to the vital organs; the result would be a slow but premature death.

So with everything in nature that is governed by the law of circulation. Any interruption of the operation of the law must be attended by unnatural and bad results.

If money is intended for circulation, the law governing it is a natural law and cannot be violated with impunity. Of course we know that money is intended for circulation as a medium of exchange for convenience only. It saves the farmer much trouble he would otherwise have in trading his products for groceries, clothing, farming machinery, etc. It saves an interminable round of "swapping," which on a large scale would be impracticable, if not impossible.

But by common consent, expressed by the stamp of the government on the coin or paper, money is taken in exchange for everything salable, and in turn used to purchase everything purchasable. So money is a mere convenience, and of itself as money has no value. To be of any value money must be active—pass from hand to hand in exchange for commodities and articles of use. When hoarded, and so long as it remains so, it can have no possible value whatever.

What then is wealth? It consists of all things that in some way by their use sustain life or add to our real comforts, be they physical, intellectual, or moral. Money of itself can serve none of these purposes. By reason of its purchasing power it merely represents wealth, and may be used as an exchange for things we wish.

As the medium of exchange money could not fill its allotted sphere of usefulness unless it were put into circulation. In the natural order of trade every man is of necessity a purchaser. Under the monetary system he must have money with which to make purchases. So if we as a people are prosperous, money must pass freely from hand to hand, and enough of it to meet all the requirements of business and trade, besides insuring employment to all at a reasonable share of the products of their labor. When money has done all this it has free circulation and is fulfilling its mission of usefulness.

Now let us see what is the true basis of the free circulation of money.

The first principle consists in its unchecked distribution. Now this cannot be if a considerable part of it is absorbed by corporations, trusts, syndicates, middlemen, and stock-jobbers generally. If these institutions hoard vastly more than they expend, then they are a hindrance to the free distribution of money. As, in the case of the circulation of moisture, if a considerable part of all the moisture evaporated from the earth were absorbed and precipitated into the ocean, there would be famine in the land, so there is a money famine when the various associations of millionaires absorb much of the money and deposit it in banks or use it to widen and deepen the sea of their own selfish speculations.

Such speculations consist largely in impoverishing the producing classes by cornering the markets for their products. And when the markets are cornered the great class of non-producers, or consumers, pay the tax thus levied by these money-gamblers. At present the producers, the farming classes everywhere, are becoming impoverished because of low prices paid for their products, while the consumers of all large cities pay high prices for the same products. Thus the money and the products of the soil are alike cornered, which effectually forces producers and consumers alike into a corner. In a word, capital has cornered the money, wealth, and products of the country, and the people are awaking to find themselves "in a hole."

Now let us follow the laws of nature into the business world, and we shall see that there is no break in their operations. Beginning where all wealth is produced, we notice that the producing classes are the great purchasers of the goods and material

Circuit of business— circulation of money.

24 NATURAL LAW

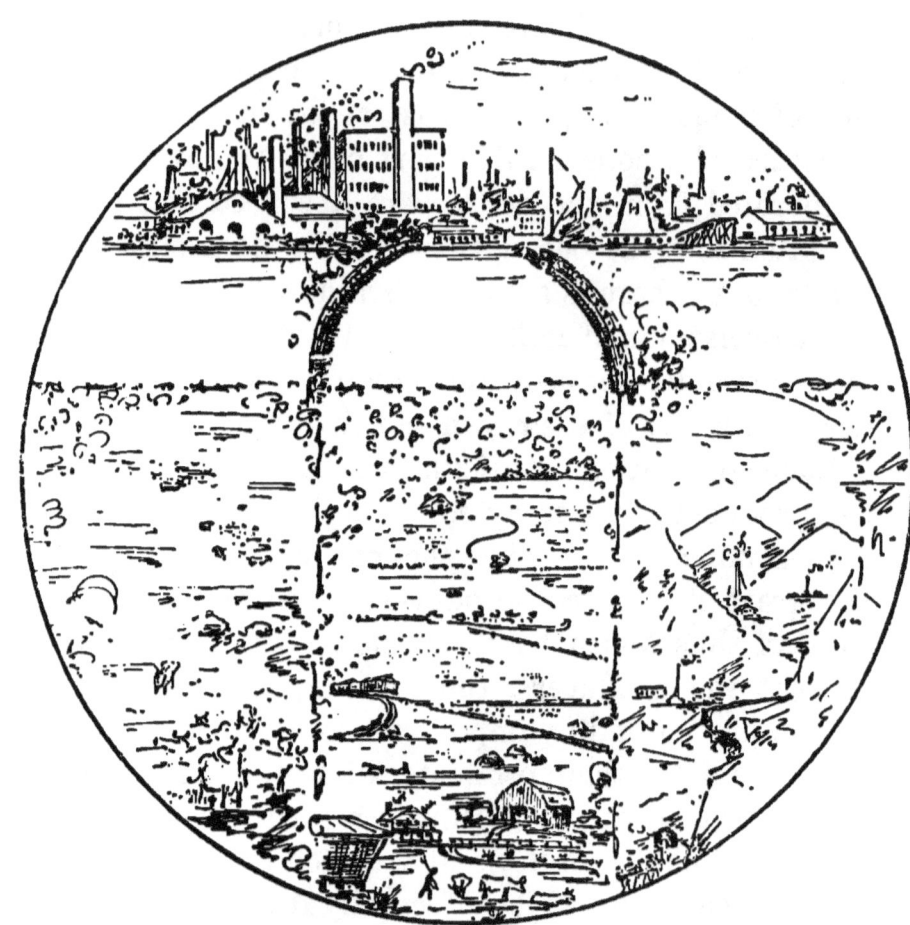

Explanation of Fig. 2.

The annexed cut (Fig. 2) is from an original drawing, and is aimed to give a general idea of the circuit of business and trade, around which active money circulates. To plainly illustrate the principle, the manufacturing and producing interests are set apart in the above illustration, the manufacturing at the top, and the producing interests—divided into three grand divisions, viz., stock-raising, agriculture, and mining—at the bottom of the cut. Between the two and across the open space the two railroad trains indicate the business circuit, one being headed toward the manufacturing, the other furnished by the manufactories and shops. These goods and material furnish the main stock in trade toward the producing, sections, the direction in which the trains are headed indicating a circuit of transportation, trade, traffic, and travel. Take your pencil and trace a line in the above cut indicated by the direction of the train leaving the manufacturing section, and the line will form a loop through the producing sections, which, including the trains, forms the business circuit.

Under our present financial system a double standard is absolutely essential to a stable currency, that should be free from disturbing fluctuations. The most of the gold should be at the great manufacturing points, and the large volume of silver at the producing points, of the business circuit. Thus, with our financial system resting upon two points of support,—free coinage of gold and silver at the ratio of 16 to 1,—a just equilibrium of currency could be maintained. The tendency of one to appreciate in value would be held in check by the other. If, for instance, from any cause gold should become scarce, silver would be available to assist in maintaining a normal circulation. If, on the other hand, silver should become scarce, gold could be used to assist silver at the producing points to carry on local traffic and trade. In either case the just equilibrium of the standards would be restored speedily—provided always that no powerful combination were allowed to destroy the money value of one or the other of the metals. After over twenty years' organized fight against silver, such a combination of capitalists, aided by legislation and finally by the general government, succeeded in forcibly removing the silver support of our financial system, effectually destroying the equilibrium of the circulating currency and all legitimate business and trade as well. When the silver support of the business circuit was removed, that point dropped about fifty per cent. ("50-cent dollar"), and the gold point was thereby forced upward at about the same per cent. elevation.

of all mercantile lines. The merchant, whether he deals in dry goods, groceries, hardware, farming implements, or whatever else, understands that his stock is the output of factories and shops. All the raw material which is made merchantable in manufactories and shops is purchased of the producing classes. Thus we see that all business and trade, including farms, mines, factories, and shops of every kind and description, form a perfect circuit, and the money that keeps the vast machinery of the business of the country going passes around this circuit and is therefore in circulation. It is in free circulation when it follows this fixed circuit of business without interruption.

There is an eternal round of dependencies of one upon the other—of the non-producer upon the producer for his products, which are to the non-producer the necessaries and luxuries of life, and of the producer upon the non-producer for money, which he gives in exchange for the products. Each toils for the other—the non-producer for the money which he must pay for the products of the producer, and the producer for the products which he exchanges for the money of the non-producer.

Now the point in the circuit where, to use an electrical term, business and trade are generated is where all the raw material that makes business and trade possible is produced. The products of the soil and earth (which includes the mines) constitute the sum of the raw material of all wealth. The producing classes exchange their raw materials for money and then pay out the money for the same materials after they have passed through the manufactory, shop, or other institution for shaping or refining the same. All the expenses of the producer are reckoned as the cost of producing the raw material. These expenses are the prices the producer pays for the material which has come back to him after it has been manufactured.

Now, when the prices the producers pay for this material remain approximately the same, or stationary, and the prices they receive for the raw material decline, they are forced to retrench in their expenses. This means that they buy less of the manufactured or refined material, which proportionally gluts the market for the same. If the prices received for the raw material decline below the cost of production, the producing classes become impoverished and are necessarily light purchasers. This tends to paralyze manufacturing industries and materially reduces the *quantity* of raw material purchased for manufacturing purposes. Thus a great per cent. of manufactured articles accumulate on the hands of the manufacturer, and the raw material on the hands of the producer.

A panic follows. Labor is thrown out of employment by the closing of manufactories, shops, mines, and the enforced idleness of the farm. All lines of trade in the great business circuit suffer alike. None escape but the speculators, who have formed trusts and combines in nearly all material, both raw and manufactured. By these trusts and combines they have taken the lion's share of all profits in coin, and stored the coin in vaults and banks as a reserved fund with which to further enforce their extortions.

For three years past the prices paid for raw material have been little above, and for some products even below, the cost of production. The prices paid for most manufactured goods and articles have remained during that time about stationary. The result is, manufacturers are overstocked with goods and the producing classes proportionally overstocked with raw material. As all business and trade complete the circuit of which the producing and manufacturing classes form a part, so they have suffered proportional losses. There is a general complaint of the scarcity of money and hard times. The circulating currency has been depleted until there is not enough to transact the regular business of the country. Thousands are going into bankruptcy.

Meantime, all the great vaults and banks are full of money: sixty-five clearing-house banks of New York City now have on deposit $548,038,200; other cities, $10,000,000, $20,000,000, $50,000,000, $100,-000,000! Banks and vaults overstocked with money, factories and shops overstocked with goods and all other articles of trade, and farms overstocked with products! Take the money out of the banks and vaults and put it into circulation, and—do you say it would bring permanent prosperity to the country? Let us see. How did such vast sums of money get out of circulation and into the vaults and banks? Who put them there? Why, speculators, of course. They have banded together and with their combined capital cornered the markets. All their profits, which are enormous and always in coin, go into vaults and banks. And so long as these speculators are allowed to control the markets, so long will money continue to go out of circulation by the millions annually. Hence it will be readily seen that, even if the speculators would throw every dollar out of their vaults and banks into circulation, and still retain control of the markets, it would be only a matter of time when they would have every dollar of it back again, and the people complaining bitterly of another panic.

These trusts and combines, numbering over one hundred and thirty, are composed of a large majority of the wealthiest men in the United States and Europe. They control the markets for the very good reason that they control the circulating currency. They oppose free coinage of silver because they want to keep free money scarce, that they may continue their uninterrupted control of the markets.

It was not merely to defeat the free-silver movement, however, that they contributed so heavily to the campaign fund. It was to defeat the great reform movement. Free silver was only the shadow of the ghost that haunted them. They saw in it a mighty movement against the unwarranted and unjust encroachments of capital on the rights and liberties of the people. It was a question of life or death to these, and so with their millions they deceived, purchased, intimidated, and coerced their way to victory.

They now have the machinery of government in

their own hands—the army, the navy, the United States treasury, the banks, with money enough to control the legislation and the wealth of the nation.

Other great checks on the free circulation of money are railroad, telephone, telegraph, and street-car corporations. These corporations rely upon the great common people for their vast income.

<small>Government ownership of railroads, telegraph, and telephone.</small>

Dividends aggregating millions of dollars are declared by these great corporations annually, and every dollar taken out of actual circulation. It requires no statistics to prove that but a very small proportion of the gross earnings finds its way back into the legitimate channels of circulation. Why? Because these corporations have long since practically completed the construction of new roads and lines, and are retrenching in their expenditures, even to forcing the wages of their employés down to the lowest point. When railroads, telephone and telegraph lines were under construction millions of dollars were thrown into circulation annually instead of being taken out, as is the case at this time.

True, these are legitimate and necessary conveniences. Rapid travel, transportation, and communication are indispensable to the present conditions and institutions of civilization. They are, indeed, the forerunners of civilization. And yet, when controlled by men who operate them with a view to personal gain only, and in the face and defiance of natural laws, they become a curse. To make them a blessing it is only necessary to remove the incentive to personal gain. The railroads, telephone and telegraph lines are public conveniences and should not be operated for private gain. Being public conveniences, they should be public property, owned, controlled, and operated by the general government upon the same principle as the United States mail. In this way, not only would personal greed be eliminated from the control and operation of these public conveniences, but the great reduction in fares, freights, telephone and telegraph service would aggregate an enormous sum annually, a sum that under the present system is taken out of actual circulation. No company of individuals will operate railroads, telephone and telegraph lines without returns in the shape of dividends. Neither would a company of individuals operate the United States mail without personal gain. If a corporation had full charge of the United States mail a two-cent stamp would not carry a letter to any part of the United States, as it now does. Instead, the cost of a letter-stamp would be at least five cents. It will be seen that the private sinking-fund in the case of corporate control of the United States mail system would be enormous, and everybody who bought stamps would contribute to that fund, just as everybody who pays fares, freights, or sends telephone or telegraph messages now contributes to the sinking-fund of millionaire stockholders, who compose the corporations operating these great public conveniences. By their government ownership, however, this vast sinking-fund, which is "net earnings" drawn directly from all classes of people, would be kept in the legitimate arteries of circulation.

The municipal ownership of street-car systems is equally urgent as viewed from the standpoint of national economy. In all the large cities the annual net earnings of street-car corporations are enormous.

<small>Municipal ownership of street-car lines.</small>

The street-car fare of five cents is a small amount to almost every one who wishes to ride on street-cars, but the grand aggregate of all the five-cent fares paid to all the street-car corporations of a large city in a single day is a big sum of money. And I am sure if that sum had to come out of the pockets of fewer people, say at the rate of twenty-cent fares, there would be an immediate demand for a reduction of fares. As it is, "what is everybody's business is nobody's business." The five-cent fares are paid, nobody kicks, and the work of tapping the arteries of financial circulation goes steadily on.

Cities could operate their street-car lines on two-cent fares, which would save hundreds of thousands of dollars annually to their circulating-fund. And the more money in circulation the greater the general prosperity.

I merely suggest, as others have done, the government ownership of railroads, telephone and telegraph lines, and municipal ownership of street-car systems as the only feasible remedy for the many evils attending their corporate or individual control. My purpose here is to point out the one great evil—that of taking in the shape of fares, freights, and message fees vast sums of money out of actual circulation, to hoard in banks or to use in so-called speculation, which means to open wider the arteries of financial circulation where they are already tapped, or to tap them in new places.

Taking money out of circulation is an evil, because it tends to impoverish the people and retard the general progress of the country. The purpose involved in taking money out of circulation has much to do with the enormity of the evil. In the poverty of excuses for private ownership of railroads, telephone and telegraph lines, and street-car systems, it is urged that they are public conveniences and in our national and commercial growth have become public necessities.

This much cannot be said, however, in behalf of the numerous combines, trusts, etc., that suck the financial life-blood of the nation without giving anything whatever in return. And right here we have another law of nature, that lies behind the natural law of circulation, which in mechanics is known as the law of mechanical equivalents, and in business is termed "value received." A stone thrown upward will fall back in the same time, with the same velocity, and strike the ground with the same force with which it was sent upward. In falling the stone takes on the same amount of energy with which it parted in going upward. Upon this principle the rigid equilibrium of matter and force is maintained. Nature requires measure for measure—value received.

in exact quantity. The ocean currents carry the warm water of the equatorial belt to polar regions, and from the polar regions is returned to the equator the exact quantity of water. This is a perpetual round and is necessary in order to maintain an equilibrium of matter. The stone gathering the same quantity of force in falling that it spends in its passage upward is necessary in order to maintain the equilibrium of force. The electric current must have a return circuit, because the quantity of electricity given out at one pole must be returned to the opposite pole of the battery or dynamo. This is why the electric current always measures the same at every point of the circuit.

This is an inexorable law of nature, and holds in commerce, trade, and finance. The law can be violated, but not with impunity. An obstruction to the circulation of sap in a tree or of blood in an animal will show its effects in the abnormal development or death of the tree or animal. Obstructions may be placed in the way of the circulation of money, but the results will inevitably show themselves in panics and, unless the obstruction be removed, in national disaster and ruin.

I wish to speak now of things that are the worst forms of obstructions to the free circulation of money. I have already alluded to them as combines, trusts, middlemen, etc.

Evil effects of trusts, combines, etc.

Railroads give you a ride or send your freight, and telephone and telegraph companies will send your messages when charges are paid; but the trusts and middlemen get your money and give you nothing in return. The trust puts up the price on coal, kerosene, or other necessaries of life, and the consumer pays the tariff out of the money in circulation. True, he gets his coal, kerosene, or other article, just as the man who pays charges gets his ride, his freight shipped, or his telephone or telegraph message sent. But there is this important difference: the coal, kerosene, or other article can be handled successfully and at less cost to the consumer without the interposition of trusts or middlemen. Unless the government operate railroads, the telephone, and the telegraph, they of necessity must be operated by companies. Not so in handling marketable commodities. They could be shipped to dealers, who could supply the public, and save to the consumers vast sums of money annually now paid to swell the hoarded millions of greedy trusts and middlemen. They are worse than drones in the great hive of human industry, for drones are said to be of some use. But these financial leeches sap the life-blood of the nation from its arteries of circulation. They place themselves between the producer and the consumer, paying the producer starvation prices and charging the consumer "all the traffic will bear." In this way the markets are practically controlled. The rivalry between the "bulls and bears" is but a system of reckless gambling in the necessaries of life. The market for products goes up or down, depending only on which of these two beasts of gambling is most powerful or adroit in scheming. The producer toils on, taking for his pay the pennies that fall from these gamblers' tables as pay for his products. The gamblers hoard their millions, which by scheming they have taken out of circulation, making money scarce, which raises its purchasing power. In time they have a corner on money itself, just as they have at this writing, four days before the presidential election of 1896. Such harmful institutions of gambling should be abolished outright. Rigid laws against all manner of gambling or wholesale speculating in the necessaries of life should be adopted and enforced. Such laws should be sweeping in effect. No person or persons should be allowed to stand between the producer and the consumer and force down the price on the one and up on the other. There should be no interference with legitimate speculation, but there should be laws against extortion. All our laws should be based upon natural laws, which exact measure for measure, no more, no less. Business and trade should be conducted upon the principle and basis of value received, which is the counterpart of the natural law of measure for measure. Upon this principle and basis nature maintains an equilibrium of matter and force, and upon this basis alone can national and international finance, commerce, and trade maintain a just equilibrium.

Money is a convenient medium of exchange for all things purchasable, and as such is the standard of values. Therefore, when money, no matter how small the amount, changes from one person to another, there should be a return of value to the person paying out the money. Putting the proposition scientifically, suppose the amount paid in this case to be one dollar, and that one dollar is the unit of value. *"Value received" a law of nature.* Now the work to be performed by the dollar should be equal to the unit of value, and this we will call a unit of work. Suppose there is nothing returned for the dollar. It has changed hands without doing any work and is therefore, as the electrician would term it, on dead-short circuit. A battery, dynamo, or any other electrical contrivance does no work when on short circuit. So long as the dollar circulates without doing its unit of work it is on short circuit. In mechanics this means to run machinery at full capacity without making it do any work. Now there is a unit of work and a unit of capacity for work, and these should be equal. The unit of work done is termed the mechanical equivalent of the unit of capacity. All machinery and appliances should be operated upon this principle, i.e., the unit of work done should be equal to the unit of capacity for doing the work. In finance, let the dollar represent the unit of capacity for doing work. Its mechanical equivalent is the unit of value which should be given in exchange for the unit of work. The unit of capacity and the unit of work should be alike fixed and unvarying. This is a law of nature. The capacity should not be greater than the work to be done, nor the work to be done greater than the capacity.

The capacity of the dollar for doing work is regulated by the number of dollars in actual circulation, or, in other words, by the law of supply and demand. It is apparent, then, that for the dollar to have a fixed unit of value there should be an approximately fixed number of dollars in actual circulation.

At this writing the number of dollars in circulation has depleted to where a gold dollar has about one and four fifths units of capacity for work; that is, the purchasing power of a dollar is about four fifths greater than it should be. The result is, products are cheap because money is dear, which is causing bankruptcy among the producers of wealth. Yes, we hear of the bankruptcy of producers everywhere, and along with it the complaint of consumers living in large cities and towns of high prices for products. This is easily explained: the middlemen and railroad corporations are between the producers and the consumers, taking the lion's share. The railroads have a corner on transportation, and the middlemen have a corner on the markets. If the consumer could purchase products direct from the producer at the prices he now has to take, the cost of living to the consumer would be reduced about one half. If, on the other hand, the consumer had free access to the producer and paid him the prices for his products he now pays for them, the producer would soon be able to pay off the mortgage on his farm.

If the unit of value or purchasing power of the dollar is nearly double what it should be because of the scarcity of dollars in actual circulation, then to increase the number of dollars in circulation would lower the purchasing power of the dollar to the normal merit. It would; but the unit could not be maintained while the railroads continued to hold a corner on transportation and the middlemen a corner on the markets, unless the number of dollars in circulation were increased at the ratio of the number of dollars hoarded by railroad corporations and middlemen. A moment's thought right here will convince any one that the free coinage of silver without free circulation would be no lasting remedy for financial difficulties and panics. Much more money would be thrown into circulation and there would be an era of more prosperous times, but with the depletion of currency continuing, and increasing with the increasing wealth and arrogance of railroad corporations and of middlemen, the era of prosperity would be brief, terminating in another mighty panic.

As a matter of fact, the government ownership of railroads, telephone and telegraph lines, and the abolition of trusts, combines, all wholesale speculations in the necessaries of life, and the restoration of silver to its proper place with gold, would settle all financial difficulties. Then the cost of transportation would be greatly reduced, and all products would find their way through a free market to the consumers; and, what is more, the vast sums of money hoarded by railroad, telephone and telegraph corporations, trusts, combines, etc., would soon be thrown back into active circulation. The dollar, whether silver or gold, would then have its true unit of value, and the nation would be financially independent and prosperous.

Nature smiles with plenty and showers her choicest gifts everywhere. If the people, by improvidence or a failure to assert their rights, allow these gifts to fall into the lap of luxury, then nature is not to blame. *Nature denies man the right to rule.* She provides abundance, and every human being is entitled to a just share. Call this socialism if you will, but there is no denying the great truth. The theory of special privileges grew out of human greed for property or power or for both. No man has the natural right to abuse authority which he has over his fellow-men, any more than he has to abuse his right to property by oppressing others. Men may have the divine right to lead or, what is much the same, serve, but no man ever had, nor ever will have, the divine right to rule. Moses led, and a greater than he proclaimed this great underlying principle of human liberty, which is recorded in Mark x. 42–45: "But Jesus called them to Him, and saith unto them, Ye know that they which are accounted to rule over the Gentiles exercise lordship over them; and their great ones exercise authority upon them. But so shall it not be among you: but whosoever will be great among you, shall be your minister: and whosoever of you will be the chiefest, shall be servant of all. For even the Son of man came not to be ministered unto, but to minister, and to give His life a ransom for many."

Moses was given the Ten Commandments, which conform perfectly to natural law. Moses was not above the law of the Ten Commandments. It has been given to no man to be above and independent of the laws which govern his subjects. There have been and are rulers, but they have been and will continue to be dethroned until human liberty will be universal. Nature has set her seal of condemnation against arbitrary forms of government where rulers are not subject to the laws they enforce on others. Moses was subject to the law of the Ten Commandments, and Jesus Christ was subject to all the laws of Christianity. And I speak reverently when I say that God holds the laws of the universe and of His being inviolate. It may be said that by these laws He governs and is governed, and the Bible assures us that by obedience to these laws we may have fellowship with Him, which shows that the Creator is not above the creature when the creature conforms to the laws of the Creator.

TRUE RELATIONS OF LAND, LABOR, AND CAPITAL

A BODY at rest remains at rest unless acted on by some external force.

This is the law of inertia and is a portion of Newton's fundamental law of motion. Common observation teaches us that with reference to any portion of earth and all bodies on its surface this law of inertia holds good. The solid body of the earth, its seas, oceans, rivers, and land, would remain motionless and changeless forever unless acted on by external forces. The force of the winds, acting upon the waters of the seas and oceans, rolls them into mountain billows, and the force of the volcano and earthquake raise and sink islands and continents, while the physical forces of man, directed by the will, raise the dead materials of the earth into shapely forms for human habitations. The clay of which the brick is formed, the stones of the vast quarries, the metals adapted to the uses of the architect and machinist, and the forests that furnish the material for building and architectural finish, would all remain shapeless in their places forever unless acted on by the forces put into operation by the human will. The hands are the instruments upon which these forces act, and in obedience to the will, under the control of purposes, the hands develop the raw materials of nature into all the various articles and things that bear the trade-mark of human design and ingenuity. The processes of development are termed labor, and all material growth and advancement are said to be the products of labor.

Labor, then, lies next to nature and should rank first on the human side in the principles of political economy. On nature's side is land, which holds in store all products and resources, and all the laws and conditions governing their proper development and use.

Having cleared away the rubbish of argument that deals with the confused and complicated effects of the operation of human institutions and laws, which are established and perpetuated in violation of natural law, we can now see our way clearly to the first cause of all material advancement and the germ idea of politico-economic science.

I have dealt at some length elsewhere with the subject of land, showing in general outline the wise economic system in the natural formation and deposit of its wealth of resources as proved by their perfect adaptation to all the possible requirements of the human family for all time. We will now consider the processes of the development of the natural resources of the earth, beginning when they yet awaited the magical touch of labor to bring them from their hiding-place.

We have seen that a body has no power of itself to move, and that, unless acted on by some external force, it will remain at rest and motionless forever. No matter whether that body be a stone, a forest of trees, a nugget of gold, a body of coal, or nuts, berries, and fruits that grow wild in the tropics, the difference in the immediate value of all these consists in the amount of labor required to make them useful. The nuts, berries, and fruits of the tropics require no preparation, yet their use involves the labor of gathering them. The coal involves the greater labor of gathering and of the preparation of stoves and furnaces for burning. The rock requires the labor of lifting from the quarry and shaping and placing in building. Great labor is required to reduce the forest to lumber suitable for building purposes, while to insure the usefulness of the nugget of gold the ingenuity and skill of labor must be expended in perfecting delicately formed and adjusted machinery by which it is minted, when it becomes a standard of value. These things, and, indeed, all things in nature, are valueless unless acted on by the external force of labor. Values lie latent in labor and spring into being at its touch. The tropical nuts, berries, and fruits have no value to the native unless he expend the labor of gathering them for sustenance. They become valuable when gathered for use, but labor precedes and is indispensable to their use; hence their value inheres in labor. This becomes quite apparent when we come to consider the value of a piece of raw material, say of cotton. What is the basis of estimate of its value? Unless raw cotton pass through some process of manufacture by which it is woven into cloth or formed into padding for quilts, cushions, etc., it has no value. It is because it can be used for these purposes that it is valuable; so its value is entirely dependent upon the labor required to put it in shape to be used. If it is urged that the manufacturing machinery performs the greater portion of the labor, I shall insist that without labor the machinery would be of no more value than were the metals of which it is composed before they were mined from the rocks. Couple with the labor of operating the factory the succession in the various processes of labor required to first dig from the rocks the metals of which the machinery is composed; the labor expended in transporting the ore to the foundry, in melting and molding the parts, and in finishing in the machine-shops; the transportation of the parts to the place where the factory is to be erected; and, finally, the putting into place the parts which when finished form the complete manufacturing plant; and when we have added the labor of digging and the transportation of the coal from which the power for the plant is generated, we have the sum total of the labor required to change the cotton from conditional to actual value. The profits derived from the various stages of labor above enumerated, including the profits derived from the production of the cotton itself, are profits on the labor employed. The capital involved is invested in facilities to get the greatest possible results from the labor employed, and these facilities are all the creation of labor. Hence aggregations of capital are aggregations of the profits on labor.

Going back to first principles, we see that nature has done her part faithfully and well, and leaves man to perform his part according to certain definite laws and conditions which she has established. Her conditions or resources are regulated by the law of distribution, which precludes the possibility of natural monopolies. The limit of her resources is circumscribed only by the capacity of the earth. No country has the monopoly of resources. They are so distributed that one country must be dependent upon another for products and things that belong exclusively to it. This causes a state of international dependencies, which necessitates international commerce and trade. In the natural order of things, one nation cannot reduce another to a condition of servitude. The condition of master and servant, employer and employed, from individuals to nations, is the direct outgrowth of human institutions and laws, which have no precedent or justification in natural law. "All men are created free and equal" is the cardinal principle of human liberty and is backed by the law of universal liberty in nature.

The water, land, and air are made free for fishes, beasts, and fowls. They were all created free and equal. The natural resources of the earth are theirs in common, and no species among them all is endowed by nature with exclusive privileges. By reason of physical power or courage, the whale may be styled the king of the waters, the lion the king of beasts, and the eagle the king of fowls, but nature has given to them no scepter of authority by which they may subjugate their kind or deny to the weakest in the scale of creation the right to the means of independent subsistence. Upon this natural right rests the cause of human liberty. Servitude inevitably results from the subversion of this right—the right to the means of independent subsistence. And servitude is an enforced, and not a natural, condition. Men serve masters not necessarily because their masters own them as property. This is an expensive and unnecessary form of servitude or slavery. Chattel slavery involves needless cares and responsibilities. Such slaves must be cared for when sick, and a vigilance must be kept lest they escape and gain their freedom. The owner is also responsible for their acts, just as he is responsible for trespass and damage if his horses, cows, or hogs destroy property belonging to others.

Not so with that form of slavery in which the victims stand between starvation and toil for those who reap what should be the reward of their labor. There is now no escape from this form of bondage.* True,

---

* Until aggregated capital got control of the wealth and circulating currency of this country there was some recognition of the rights of the employed. Now labor is regarded as chattel, subject to the so-called law of supply and demand, which is the natural law of supply and demand complicated

the liberty of changing masters is granted, but this often means a change from bad to worse. When out of employment their labor is on the market that tends to the lowest rather than the highest bidder, if, indeed, there be a bid at all. There are no bidders now for the labor of tens of thousands in this country, who are somehow existing in enforced idleness. Cut off from means of independent subsistence, men must serve whom, when, and where they can, and when they cannot they become unwilling vagrants.

Going back once more to first principles, we find that there was a time when all men were in fact free and equal, a time when no man usurped the authority to deny to other men the right to the means of independent subsistence. That order of things was changed, and all subsequent history recites the oft-repeated story of "man's inhumanity to man." That change did not come about in the natural order of things. If that order had been maintained by all the institutions of organized society and government to the present time, such terms as "master" and "employer" would have been unknown. That order was reversed, however, by the early adoption of a monopoly rather than a coöperative system. It began when greed got the mastery of men, who usurped authority, through which they secured the exclusive privilege of unrestricted owner-

and perverted by the manipulations of greed out of all recognition. And so labor has lost all the dignity and liberty it once enjoyed, and, unless the compensation reaches the plane of "salary" or "fees," it is now considered menial.

ship. The arbitrary authority to rule was termed "the divine right of kings," and upon that assumed right hereditary offices were created, and filled by those who, by virtue of their offices, should enjoy special and exclusive privileges. Among the privileges enjoyed by this titled class was the right to the ownership of vast landed estates, which necessarily involved the servitude of the many who were thus cut off from the means of independent subsistence. The only access to the soil was in tenantry, and the tenant was and is the servant, and the landlord the master. The products of his toil are taken in rent, which is only a term for one method of creating capital from the products of labor. The other method consists in the assessment levied upon the labor of those who are employed by reason of their utter dependence for employment upon the owners of the means of subsistence. These are the two methods of creating capital, and they result, directly or indirectly, from land monopoly, which, as landlordism, has been and continues to be an underlying principle of the institutions of human government. So firmly rooted became the operation of that principle that the indiscriminate monopoly of land, with all its attendant evils, was finally regarded as the necessary and unavoidable outgrowth of all organized society and government. We have become so familiar with land and all other species of monopoly, with the accompanying system of the employment of labor and the impression that all profits are somehow derived from the things in which investments are made, that it is not easy to realize the fact that primarily all aggregations of wealth or capital are aggregations of the profits on labor.

To make this apparent it is only necessary to point out that under a coöperative system wealth could not aggregate, simply because all men would get the products of their own labor. Under such a system there could be no monopolies, for the very evident reason that monopolies are possible only through the instrumentality of wage-earners, without whose labor capital could find no profitable investment. Labor is not only "the strong right arm of capital," but it is both arms, hands, feet, body—all, absolutely all there is of active capital. A body—of land, of mineral ore, of anything valuable that can be mentioned—at rest remains at rest unless acted on by the external force of labor. If that labor can be bought and used by some one who has secured the exclusive right to the body of land, mineral ore, or other valuable thing, then, everything else being equal, it becomes profitable to the extent of the labor expended, for which he receives the profits. These profits, he ignorantly claims, are on his investment, never realizing that the means with which he made the investment were the creation of labor. As all values are the creation of labor, so all profits derived from enhanced valuations are necessarily profits on labor. So no matter if the capital of the one who makes the investment comes to him through inheritance, it nevertheless represents just so much of profits on labor stored in the successive stages of accumulations by his ancestors. No matter how or when capital is or was accumulated, it all represents the profits on labor stored in process of accumulation. It may be in the hands of a number of men by reason of their coöperative labor, or in the possession of one man, who has reaped the profits of the labor that otherwise would have been coöperative; in either event the principle is precisely the same, namely, that capital is the profits on labor stored in process of accumulation. In the rounds or evolutions of the various processes of labor, wealth is evolved, and aggregates in the hands of those who control labor. If each individual controls his own labor he receives the products thereof, to which, according to natural law, he is entitled. If, on the other hand, labor is controlled by a few, its products (wealth) aggregate in their hands, and are termed capital.

Reduced to first principles, we find that for capital to aggregate it is first necessary for a few men to control the labor of many, which is done by cutting off all access to the means of independent subsistence. The process is the monopoly of the soil and the consequent monopoly of its products. The utter dependence of the many upon the few results from the operation of arbitrary and unnatural human institutions, which create monopolies and which are and have been essentially alike in all governments, the world over, from the beginning of organized society. Malthus made the important discovery that population tends to crowd upon subsistence, but he evidently failed to make the much more important one that that tendency is entirely due to the operation of unjust human institutions already pointed out, and not to natural causes. For evils do not spring from natural causes; they are always and everywhere the legitimate fruits of violations of natural law.

It will be claimed that remedies I suggest cannot be reached by legislation, because such legislation would interfere with vested rights and there would be great opposition to such measures. There would undoubtedly be great opposition to measures for the curbing of a spoils system, but the opposition would come from the privileged classes who profit by the system. It would be urged by those classes that the purchase of railroads, for instance, would bankrupt the government.

<small>The people — the government.</small>

There is a general misapprehension of what really constitutes the government. Most people seem to regard the government as an institution above and independent of the people. They do not seem to realize that all the just powers of the government are derived from the consent of the governed; that those whom they elect to all offices, from President down to the least, are elected to do the will of the people and are therefore public servants; that the duties of these public servants are defined by the Constitution and laws, and emphasized by their solemn oath of office; that their official duties are, or should be, determined by the wishes of the people who elect them and pay for their services; that no public servant has a right to arrogate to himself the prerogative of rulership, or to set his personal opinion above the will of the people; that the salaries of all officials and all expenses of government are defrayed by the people in the shape of the various forms of taxation.

Now, therefore, it appears that it is not for any official or specially privileged class to say that any enterprise or undertaking is too expensive for the government. It is the sole right of the people to determine all matters of government policy and set the bounds to the amount of taxation they are willing to pay.

If the people wish to own and operate the railroads and make them an institution of government as they have the mail system, then who shall interfere and say that it would be too expensive? or who shall say that it would be unjust to confiscate and pay for public conveyances and appropriate them for public use? Who shall say that the public has not the right to own and operate all public conveyances and conveniences? How can this be said in the face of the unjust and exorbitant rates paid by the public to private corporations for the use of public conveyances and conveniences?

As to bankrupting the government, if the slow process of paying in fares and freights millions of dollars annually as clear profits to private railroad corporations will not bankrupt the people, it is evident that the payment of the sum of these profits for, say, ten or twenty years at once and outright for the railroads would even reduce the chances of bankruptcy. And at the expiration of the ten or twenty years, when the government bonds for the indebtedness shall have been paid and it is found that the millions spent have purchased the perpetual right to the use of railroads by the public, then would the people realize the full force and efficacy of their great stroke of national economy. For the millions paid out they would have the railroads, whereas if they pay them out as fares and freights the money goes into the vaults and safes of private corporations, representing so much clear gain to the corporations and as much loss to the people.

The government ownership of railroads is a proposition that capitalists would oppose, and ostensibly on economic grounds. They would oppose bonding the government for the vast sum required to purchase the railroads, and would strive to terrorize the people with the scarecrow of bankruptcy; but the political record of the past two or three years shows that capitalists did not hesitate to bond the government for hundreds of millions of dollars to pay for the mistakes and extravagance that have characterized the control of affairs of government for many past administrations. These millions must be paid by the people, and in the record of the expenses of government will stand as dead loss to them.

There is absolutely nothing in the way of the government ownership of railroads but the will of the people. Their decision would settle that question, as well as the question of government ownership of telephone and telegraph lines, the suppression of land monopoly, trusts, and all gambling in the necessaries and comforts of life. It is not only the prerogative of the people to do these things, but it is their duty. To put an end to all the evils of government would be but to act in accordance with "the first law of nature," which is self-preservation. It is the plain duty of the people to protect themselves as well as their property.

In a republic like our own the moral, social, political, and financial dependencies and connections are interminable. None can fully escape the effects of evils that work moral, social, political, or financial injury to any considerable number of people. For, as a rule, evils are not sectional; they are dovetailed into society, politics, and finance, and invariably tend to sap the moral foundations of government, by which they thrive and with which they fight down all opposition; and these are deception, ridicule, fraud, and force. The first of these is sophistry, by which error is adroitly substituted for the truth, or the truth perverted into the appearance of error. The second is derision, which is a powerful weapon, as it can always be effectively used by attacking personal pride and vanity. The third is bribery and the promises of office or position. The fourth is bulldozing, the boycott, intimidation, and coercion.

It is because men know that these weapons will be

used that they refuse to assert themselves against the inroads of public evils. Some men have dared to favor the government ownership of railroads, telephone and telegraph lines, but the weapon of ridicule has been applied so vigorously that the cause has gained comparatively few advocates. All these weapons are used in the defense of trusts, combines, land monopoly, etc.

How, then, can great evils be curbed or abolished? This question has been asked throughout all ages, but has never yet been experimentally answered. It involves the greatest and gravest social and political problem, and few there are who believe that it will ever be solved; and it must be confessed that the grounds for doubt are well taken. I have little hope that mankind, alone and unaided, will ever found a government whose institutions will be free from the contaminations of evils. So long as men yield to the evil instincts of their natures, so long will the evils of the individual aggregate in the association of individuals which is society; for, after all, the character of society depends upon the character of the individuals of which it is composed.

But the mistake of tolerating social and political evils is not so much the fault of moral weakness as it is a lack of proper education. The *Politics involves all personal interests.* whole question of social and political purity, while it involves moral purity, is largely a question of laudable self-interest. Our highest conception of self-interest dictates a course, in social and political as well as in the individual life, that is at once free from all evils that can bring nothing but injurious effects. It dictates rather a course characterized by temperance and the adoption of the golden rule in all the practical affairs of life. And the golden rule itself is a natural law, since it expresses an eternal principle of justice. It is also a sublime conception of self-interest, since a society or government founded upon that one rule of action would enjoy the most perfect preservation of the rights and interests of each and all. Such a society or government would certainly enjoy a perfect immunity from evils. Self-interest alone would dictate their exclusion. The education of the people of such a society or government would be such as to fully enlighten them on the disastrous effects of evils, and, if from no other cause than the desire to promote their own best interests, they would repel all evils at the first suggestion of their approach.

An appeal for social and political purity, then, is an appeal to the self-interest of all classes of people, from the pauper to the multimillionaire. I sometimes think the millionaire bears the greatest burden of all human responsibility: in his mind, the burden of worrying over interminable business complications; on his heart and conscience, the burden of the injustice his business methods too frequently work; and in his judgment, the burden of consciousness that all with him is, after all, only "vanity and vexation of spirit." This was the bitter experience of him who was the wisest and wealthiest of his day and age. After experiencing the intoxicating effects of boundless wealth and power, even Solomon, in all his glory, cried out at last, in the anguish of bitter remorse and disappointment, "All is vanity and vexation of spirit." I have known many who enjoyed a large measure of happiness in comparative poverty, but I have known or heard of but one happy millionaire. Then it were better for the millionaire that he remove from himself all that robs him of that greatest of all human blessings—happiness. Blinded by his lust for gold, he does not realize while in the heat of his struggles for the accumulation of wealth that he is rapidly disqualifying himself for all real enjoyment. He does not seem to know that he is passing through a hardening process by spurning sentiment and crushing out all the higher sensibilities of his nature. He may have never thought that real enjoyment comes, not in the mere possession of things we call wealth, but in their proper use. Indeed, the fierce desire for wealth seems to hold its subject by a sort of hypnotic spell, which subdues the will and drives the willing captive through all his arduous and fruitless toil of years. Some, and it may be many, are not freed from the spell until, like Solomon, they drink the bitter dregs that ever lie at the bottom of the cup from which the rich must drink, and then at last, in Solomon's galling words, they cry, "All is vanity and vexation of spirit." I appeal to the inner consciousness of the millionaire for an admission of the truth of what I have here written.

And yet I would not be understood as standing opposed to the just accumulation of wealth. An ample competency is desirable and could never interfere with the rights of any. But I stand on the basis of natural laws backed by all experience when I say that all who strive for more than an ample competency are pursuing a course that is opposed to their own best interests.

If we turn to all other classes of people—the struggling, toiling millions—and ask them *why* they struggle and toil, some of them will tell us that they are in pursuit of wealth, while the vast majority will declare that it is because of sheer necessity. Ask them why it is a necessity, and they will answer that others have possession of all the money and wealth and that they are compelled to toil for them for subsistence. Ask them if they have any choice in the matter, and they will answer no. Ask them if they have a hope of sometime owning a home or having a competency, and you will astonish them. Ask them why others have all the wealth and money, and they cannot tell you. If you suggest to them that it is all their own fault, that they as citizens and voters have permitted various usurpations on their rights and have consented to the establishment and promotion of evils that are the direct cause of all their poverty, some, more ignorant, will doubt the truth of your statement, while others will admit that they know it, but affirm their helplessness in the matter. Few there are in all this nation who, knowing of the evils that corrupt society and politics and cause all the poverty and misery in the nation, know that it is by the consent of the people that they exist. The consent may consist in a passive acquiescence in, or time-serving obedience to, existing institutions. But in a nation of citizens and voters, whose will is the law, subserviency is consent.

I lay the blame at the door of every intelligent citizen and voter. He should know that every condition and institution of evil is against his own best interest and that it is his duty as well as his right to abolish it. He should know that it is a matter of self-defense as well as the defense of others, and that all voters, individually and collectively, are bound by all the ties of citizenship and of loyalty to their own interests to strike down the evils that corrupt society, politics, and government.

<small>The duty of the people.</small>

Let no man be so foolish as to believe that he is out of the reach of public evils, for even the rich are affected by them. Especially are they, sooner or later, affected by the evils they inflict upon the people. History tells us that time and again they have returned to them in the forms of devastating wars and revolutions.

The human family is bound together by mutual ties of one common interest as closely as are members of one body. Take, for example, your own body. If you but injure one member, if you but crush one bone, every nerve of your body will thrill, every fiber of your being will suffer in unison. The lifeblood circulating through the veins and arteries will carry the tidings of distress from the injured part to all other parts of the body, and all suffer in turn. And so with the human family. We are members one of another and mutually dependent upon one another. "The hand cannot say to the foot, I have no need of thee;" neither can the rich say to the poor, "I have no need of thee." While some parts of the body are not so comely as other parts, yet they are equally useful, and if the uncomely parts suffer, so also must the comely suffer with them. And so the rich cannot oppress the poor and cause them to suffer without suffering in turn. As the blood carries the injury to all parts of the body, so the life-giving principle that flows through the tide of humanity will bring back upon the oppressor the result of his oppression.

Blinded as they are by greed and lust for power, I can understand why the rich oppress the poor and are indifferent to all their demands for justice and fair play. But I cannot comprehend the depths of selfishness of men who are *fairly* prosperous and who side with the rich in their policy of oppression. The depths of their folly in resting in the false security of the belief that they are so far above the poor that they are beyond the reach of oppression are simply incalculable. They should know that as the rich become richer the poor become poorer, and that the ranks of the poor are continually recruited from among those who are falling on every hand before the fierce exactions of combined wealth. From 1890 to 1896, both inclusive, the sifting process of our financial system has made tramps of thousands of laborers, and laborers of thousands of men who had homes or who were engaged in lucrative businesses or professions. Farmers have become homeless and penniless, and their lands have invariably gone into the hands of moneyed men or banking institutions. Merchants and business men have failed, and their places have been taken by large moneyed concerns. Vast moneyed interests are fast absorbing the trade of the country, and the time seems to be at hand when the independent business men in our large cities who are not backed by capital will be forced out of business by the fierce competition of larger moneyed concerns.

More than fifteen years ago Henry George, that fearless champion of human liberty and one of the world's most gifted thinkers and writers, startled the world with his aggressive announcement that "the rich are becoming richer and the poor poorer," and in the face and opposition of the rich laid the blame at their doors. The events from the time that the world first read "Progress and Poverty" down to the present have strengthened the unanswerable argument of Mr. George. Indeed, he did not then see or picture the worst. And it is well that he did not. Had he foreseen the presidential election of 1896, which resulted in the political domination of plutocracy, his mighty genius would have lacked the enthusiasm essential to the work of a great reformer. Had he seen the methods and means employed to bring about that result, how could he have voluntarily enlisted in what now seems the thankless and fruitless work of reform?

Oh, the appalling spectacle of American citizens falling prostrate before the plutocratic weapons of deception, ridicule, fraud, and force! And that, too, when our election laws guarantee the secrecy of the ballot! The cowardice that would cringe and cower under the display of these weapons when human liberty is at stake is unworthy of the slave to whom liberty is but a dream, much more of the men who boast that they are citizens and rulers of the greatest republic on earth. Away with such boasting! Let neither these, nor those who ignorantly serve the money power with all the kingly wealth of their citizenship, boast, but rather let them hide their heads in shame when the sad story is told of the defeat of popular government in 1896.

These are the elements that most threaten the perpetuity of our free institutions—the cowardice and ignorance of voters. I had thought to favor the adoption into law of the initiative and referendum, by which the republic would easily change from a representative to a popular form of government, but this reform can come only through the political education of the voters.

The policy and course of the administration that will expire on the 4th of March, 1897, has proved that representatives may easily become dictators and oppressors. The President, with his unrestricted power of appointment to and removal from offices of great honor and trust, may use that power as a lash to compel an army of official appointees to side with and assist him in the nefarious work of undermining the liberties of the people. Backed by the combined wealth of the nation, and with the army and navy at his command, he can disregard laws that hamper his dictatorship, violate others by unwarranted federal interference, and by persistently degrading silver from its proper money standard deplete the currency, which impoverishes the people; heavily bond what is left of the wealth of the nation to syndicates, whose dictations in finance are implicitly followed, the President may easily become the dictator. Such is the record of the last administration, and the President may truly be said to have been the dictator whose reign was limited to four years. Then, "by the will of the people," he is to be succeeded by an oligarchy whose power to further impoverish the people, and render them still more impotent to battle against the weapons of plutocracy four years hence, shakes all confidence in the ability of the people for self-government!

That confidence cannot be revived unless the politically ignorant, cowardly, and dishonest can be educated up to a knowledge of what really constitutes their own best interests. These people must learn that their liberties are never safe unless they are in their own keeping. They must learn that the interests of the rich are not in keeping with their own, and that the rich are keeping a sharp lookout for their own best interests. It is a simple lesson in politics that men's ideas of proper legislation depend largely on the nature of their own personal interests. If rich, their ideas of proper legislation are in the interest of the rich; if a producer, then in the interest of the producing classes and, incidentally, all other classes of the common people; if a lawyer, then to complicate our laws and render it impossible for every man to be his own lawyer; if a politician or demagogue, why, always in the interest of the biggest pull or the most "boodle" for himself. But it should be known that the most unsafe representatives of the people are from the ranks of the rich, the legal profession, and professional politicians.

Now every voter knows what self-interest means, but many are too often short-sighted. The politically ignorant think it is to their interest to give out the impression that they herd with the rich, although all their interests are on a plane with the interests of the great common people. The cowardly through fear would rather run the risk of sacrificing their liberties than to risk being discharged or being otherwise temporarily thrown out of employment; or he may be a business man, and afraid of the boycott; a farmer, and afraid of a merciless creditor. But, whatever the occupation, he should bear in mind that liberty is priceless and that no sacrifice is too great to give in exchange for it. You may keep your position if you are a toiler, your business if you are a business man, your farm if you are a farmer; but when your liberties are gone you will find that your employment is gone or your pay reduced to the point of starvation, your store is gone because you could not compete with rich concerns, and that your farm is gone, like thousands more, into the great holdings of land monopolists.

In one of his speeches, Patrick Henry, the great orator of the Revolution, said, "Give me liberty, or give me death!"

This is the pledge of the signers of the Declaration of Independence: "We mutually pledge to each other our lives, our fortunes, and our sacred honor." Pledged to uphold the declarations of liberty and independence embodied in that sacred document, they stood ready with their lives, their fortunes, and their honor as a sacrifice, if need be, for the people of the colonies, who looked to them for deliverance from British oppression.

"Sink, swim, live or die, survive or perish, I am for the Declaration." This was said by a patriot who urged the adoption of the Declaration of Independence. The prospect of losing property, honor, or life itself had no terrors for our forefathers, who preferred death to bondage under British rule. And yet British rule would have been no more oppressive and cruel than the oppression of plutocracy that now threatens our liberties.

But what shall we say of the dishonest—the citizen and voter who will sell his vote for a few paltry dollars? What can be said in apology for a man who is so dead to principle and every instinct of manhood, so blind to his own highest and best interests, as to barter away for a pittance the only safeguard of his liberties? Is it enough to say that he has sunk to the lowest depths of dishonor and deserves the execration of all his fellows? Shall we add more and say that he is unworthy of the exalted privilege of citizenship and should be disfranchised? Let me say that he should not be permitted to heap dishonor upon the sacred cause of human liberty. He should be hunted down and convicted of high treason against his country and banished forever from its shores. High treason? Yes; he has conspired against every sacred institution of his country, bartering away to greater conspirators that which must affect the destiny of his fellow-citizens as well as his own. As the liberties of all depend upon the votes of all, so the ballot is not the exclusive property of any. A voter has the exclusive right to cast his ballot as he will, but when it is cast it is no longer his. It becomes the property of the State or nation, and is a unit of force which shall determine the character of government, it may be, for all time. A vote cannot contribute to the undermining of the liberties of the voter who cast it without contributing to the same extent in undermining the liberties of all other voters, including their wives and children; therefore should the sanctity of the ballot be preserved by the manhood of the nation. It is the imperative duty of every honest voter to urge that the safeguard of effective laws be thrown about the ballot, that will provide for the rigid prosecution and severe punishment of criminals who sell their votes, of worse criminals who buy them, and of all other criminals who have to do with falsifying election returns. These classes of criminals and conspirators should be arraigned as traitors, tried, convicted, disfranchised, and banished. This would insure the absolute purity of elections.

There is another large class of voters, who, in view of all the political perfidy that has been practised on the people in the name of party, should be classed with the ignorant. They are those who are led and controlled by the name of party. Every intelligent voter must know that parties are made up of men with leaders who are actuated by personal ambition. There was a time in the history of this country when to faithfully serve the people was looked upon as the first and highest duty of a representative, for which service he would secure the brightest honors. With the advent of combined wealth and the money power that principle has been supplanted by bosses, who control political rings that dominate parties for the spoils of office. Money is now the dominant incentive in politics, as it is in everything else. In the early history of this republic offices often had to seek the men, whereas now the money expended to secure offices is as great, and sometimes many times greater than, the amount of regular salaries. Some office-seekers are rich and have no other desire to hold office than to dominate politics and secure legislation in the interest of the class to which they belong. Others see "boodle" ahead, and the number who grow rich in politics is evidence that they reach the goal of their ambition. The number of faithful representatives of the people is now comparatively few. Bosses and political rings have dominated the two old parties for a quarter of a century, gradually growing bolder in their methods until the presidential election of 1896, when both parties were practically dissolved. Both parties as they now stand retain the same old names, but national issues that have been maturing for years have forced themselves upon the parties and have now become party issues. The Republican party, that long since outlived its usefulness, has become the party of plutocracy. The Democratic party, that had become the party whose leaders were in office "for revenue only," arose in the might of an outraged people, formulated a new alignment of principles made up largely of old ones that the party had long since abandoned, and emerged from political chaos a reorganized party with new leaders. Many "old line" Republicans and Democrats were forced to break party lines and at the election cross-fire with their ballots. These dissenters have found out for the first time that parties can change their leaders and measures and still retain their old names, and that it is not safe to belong to the name of a party unless one stands prepared to change along with the leaders and measures.

It is to be hoped that the present breaking up of party lines will cause voters generally to be more independent and to decide once for all that they belong to no party. It is the duty as well as the privilege of every voter to advocate measures that promise the greatest good to the greatest number;

always reserving the right, however, to vote for what, in his judgment, are the best men and measures, regardless of party name. Just in proportion as voters renounce allegiance to parties and take their places as independent citizens, just in that proportion will they inform themselves on national questions touching their own best interests. Let us not forget that the cardinal principle of a republican government is "the greatest good to the greatest number." This principle should be the political straight-edge of every voter, and by it he should draw the line on men and measures before casting his ballot. In this way he will be enabled to vote for the best men and measures.

But in a representative system of government like this, with its packed conventions and political slates, it often happens that there is little real choice between the men and measures to be voted for at general elections. Such has been the predicament of voters at presidential elections for the past twenty years. Gradually party distinctions grew less, until we now have the spectacle of a Republican administration ushered into power by the help of the outgoing Democratic administration. It is needless to say that there will be no material change of the policy of the late administration. That goes without saying. And it is a matter of memory that there has been little change in the policy of administrations for the past twenty years, notwithstanding there have been four changes of party name within that time. The whole tendency of them all has been to administer the affairs of government in the interest of the rich, culminating in an unconditional surrender at the last election to that class.

It is evident, then, that so long as we maintain a representative system of government, so long will it be necessary for every honest, intelligent voter to be an agitator if he would aid in preserving the liberties of the people, which, of course, involve his own. *The people have the right to criticize faithless public servants.* In no way can a great reform be brought about except by agitation. Agitation provokes investigation, and investigation leads to a correct understanding of the matter under discussion. Every citizen and voter should be fully conscious of his power. He should know that there is absolutely no appeal from a decision of a majority of voters, of which he may be one; that it is his prerogative to criticize what he considers the unjust policy of the President, Congressmen, or even members of the Supreme Court. These are all public servants, paid for their services by the voters, for which in return they are expected to render such services as are determined by the Constitution, laws, and their solemn oath of office.

An appeal may be taken from the veto of the President to Congress and by a two-thirds vote of that body the veto set aside; a law, adopted by Congress and signed by the President, may be declared unconstitutional and set aside by the Supreme Court; but by the will of the people Presidents are unseated, Congresses changed, and even the Supreme

Court may be reorganized. Thus the will of the people is the great tribunal from whose decision no appeal can be taken.

What power, what authority, what majesty, is vested in the ballot! Then how wisely should its power, authority, and majesty be preserved! How jealously should each and every voter guard its sanctity from every suggestion of intrigue! How he should watch with jealous care this the only sure safeguard of his liberty!

BIMETALLISM.

By bimetallism is meant the free and unlimited coinage of gold and silver at a ratio determined by both the ratios of production of the two metals and the demands of commerce and trade.

Now I have made it the guide of my life to seek out the truth in all matters, and in public discussions to be sure that my conclusions accord with the truth before announcing them. I have found in all my investigations that the conditions and laws of nature form the groundwork of all truth. Error and imitation are the only things that are artificial. All art is imitation of nature; all error is counterfeit and is in conflict with nature.

I am for bimetallism not merely because it would put more money in circulation, for, as I have shown elsewhere, if the trusts and market manipulations were not abolished, simply increasing the currency would do little, if any, permanent good. But I fully indorse bimetallism because it is sustained by the conditions and laws of nature.

Now, reader, let us reason together and endeavor to reach the truth as we find it revealed in nature.

<small>Natural law and bimetallism.</small> Let us bear in mind at the outset that every impression we have that is true, every correct conclusion that we reach by reason, every idea that is founded in truth, has its counterpart in nature.

Spiritual laws, or the principles of Christianity, are but the continuation of natural laws upon a higher plane. If there be God,—and surely no intelligent being can doubt it,—then is nature "God's oldest book." The laws and conditions of nature are actuated by intelligent purpose, and all the possibilities of human intelligence and of higher civilization are absolutely dependent on the directing force of that purpose.

Behind all civilization, aye, behind creation itself, is the intelligent purpose. God created, man discovers. All that man has accomplished in his grand march toward civilization, and all that it is possible for him to accomplish, is and must be the result of his discoveries.

Going back to the Adamic period, and no matter which we accept, whether the accepted geological or the Mosaic account of creation, we find man in possession of nothing but possibilities. He had the possibilities of expanding intelligence with which to explore the hidden resources of nature and appropriate them to his various needs.

When the earth was still wrapped in the swaddling-clothes of chaos and night, before light and life had been spoken into existence, the germ of all future progress lay latent in the molten rocks, in the surging billows of the mighty deep, tossed by lurid tempests, and in the weird flame of a thousand volcanic fires set against the midnight blackness of the upper and outer darkness, awaiting the calm, the open sky, and the quickening sunlight that should follow the Laurentian storm, when "God said, Let there be light." And after the light came life—the dawn animal. Ages and eons rolled in alternate periods of light and unfolding life, with succeeding outbursts of nature's vast developing forces, until the last storm of evolution was hushed, when, behold! the earth was the fit habitation of man for all time. Man came, and since then sixty centuries of history. And now how vast the number of his descendants, how splendid the evidences of his progress and civilization! How the earth and the air teem with life—vegetable, animal, human! The germ of the possibilities of nature has surely budded and blossomed and gives promise of ripening into fruitage. Nature speaks eloquently to man of all her secrets and wisely through her laws; but man hears little, heeds less, and rests self-satisfied in the delusion of his own conceit. Few have listened well, and they have strewn the pathway of our race-life rich with discoveries.

Nature had possibilities in store for man of not only supplying his needs, but of material wealth ample for a hundred consecutive civilizations equal to that of to-day. And before man was, nature is pregnant with these possibilities. Behind the possibilities of both man and nature is prophecy; behind man the prophecy of the development of practically unlimited mental, moral, and spiritual possibilities; and behind nature resources and conditions that even now are only partially developed.

The record of discoveries and inventions (and inventions are but discoveries) marks the events in the fulfilment of the prophecy that lies behind man and nature. Science is man's effort to theoretically interpret, and history is the record of interpretation of that prophecy. Mathematics, astronomy, chemistry, geology, and natural history all unite to form one grand theory of progress. We turn for evidence to the history of all that has been really discovered and practically demonstrated, and we are convinced that the theory is correct. All progress, then, is the fulfilment of antecreation prophecy. And this prophecy was laid in the foundations and superstructure of the universe by a power directed by an intelligence as infinite in wisdom as progress is admitted to be unlimited in possibilities. Starting from the premises that the antecreation prophecy was the work of infinite intelligence and that the progress of man and nature is the practical interpretation of the prophecy, let us now read in outline a brief sketch of interpretation as gathered from the history of man and the story of the rocks.

Beginning with the advent of man in nature, we find that his needs were necessarily primitive and remained so until he discovered that nature held in store for him more than a crude hut and a bare subsistence. Here began the great era of human discoveries. Iron, coal, and copper were discovered, dug out of the rocks, and shaped into tools, which were used to chisel stones for the purpose of building houses, temples, and altars. He discovered gold and silver and used them to adorn the temples he had built and for personal ornament. He also conceived the idea of giving gold and silver a valuation, which was necessarily reckoned in measurable quantities with reference to the measurable quantities of commodities and articles of general use. This has been the basis of the valuation of gold and silver through all the ages up to the present time. In time the measurable quantity of these metals became fixed, the ratio of valuation of gold to silver being determined by the relative quantities produced. Thus the ratio at which the metals were produced determined their commercial ratio. And this ratio has been approximately maintained until of recent years, when men, actuated by greed and assuming to be wiser than nature, demonetized silver.

But let us go back to primitive man and follow him through his discoveries that have led him up to his present state of civilization.

He needed fire, and he drew it from the flint. He needed weapons for self-defense, and he placed sharpened flints in the ends of sticks for spears. He needed houses, and he discovered iron, and with it he found that stone could be chiseled in shape for building purposes. After a while he discovered copper, and then he discovered a process of hardening it into tools of superior grade. And he discovered gold, silver, and lead, and a process of melting and shaping all the metals to suit his requirements.

Gradually his capacity for the use and enjoyment of his various discoveries expanded, which in turn stimulated his desire and ambition for new discoveries. Ships were built, cities founded, and literature became the classics to which the greatest writers and authors of the ages since have turned for inspiration.

We take a leap of centuries and find man rapidly advancing to a high state of civilization. He has discovered coal, steam, and finally electricity. He uses coal to convert water into steam, and applies steam to ships and railroads.

Electricity is made to convey thought with lightning speed and to drive all manner of machinery. Continents have been discovered, great cities built, and he has put the whole earth in order for his use.

This is a rough outline of man's progress, but it will serve to impress the force of my reasoning on the mind of the reader. We have seen that the discovery and use of the metals were indispensable to man's progress. Without iron and copper material advancement would have been impossible.

And again, if iron and copper had not been stored away in the formation of the earth man would have been left without the essential elements of material advancement. But nature had them stored away, and that, too, in quantities to fill all the requirements of the most advanced civilization of all the world.

So, too, with coal. Its practically unlimited deposit proved the prophecy of the coming civilizations, and made provision for the supply of fuel that would necessarily be required. True, coal is a geological formation and is the chemical product of inundated forests; but this does not weaken the evidence of the purpose for which coal was formed. That is determined by the perfect adaptation of coal to man's requirements, and in quantities ample for all his purposes.

And looking back over the history of man's progress, we notice that the purposes to which he put all the minerals as he discovered them, although now broadened in their use, have remained unchanged. Coal may yet be supplanted by new discoveries in the application of electricity, but it is certain that until that time it will not be defuelized. Iron and copper may yet be supplanted by the scientific formation of other metals lighter and stronger, but until that time they will still be put to the uses for which they were evidently designed and will keep the place assigned them by man from their first discovery.

No metal will be thrown out of use except it be supplanted by some other metal or its equivalent. We may reach a state of civilization like that pictured by Edward Bellamy in "Looking Backward," when our present monetary system will be abandoned, but until that time neither gold nor silver will be permanently demonetized.

There is another standpoint from which we may observe that nature speaks for bimetallism. We note her indorsement from her established order of things, which is on the basis of two. By this I mean that the principle upon which the laws of nature operate involves two opposite conditions, which together produce effects. As evidence let us first take magnetism as a witness. The principle underlying magnetism is polarity, which means two opposite points termed "poles," which are indispensable to and determine the action of magnetic force. The earth is now known to be a vast magnet having two opposite magnetic poles.

Principle of bimetallism in nature.

The earth is made up of molecules, and it is by cohesion these molecules are bound together, the aggregation of which forms the body of the earth. Cohesion is magnetism acting at insensible distances. That is to say, every molecule of the earth's body is a miniature magnet with opposite poles capable of mutual attraction. The attraction of molecules, or molecular attraction, is termed "cohesion" in physics; in chemistry it is termed "chemical affinity." Hence we see that polarity, which means two opposite and unlike poles, is the basic principle of magnetism and chemistry.

Again, magnetism has two principles of action—attraction and repulsion. "Unlike poles attract; like poles repel." That is, if you bring two magnets near each other with their poles reversed they attract each other. If like poles are presented they mutually repel. Molecules, being miniature magnets, behave in the same manner when brought under chemical test. They attract or repel as their poles are unlike or like when brought into chemical touch.

The atom is the last division of matter and possesses all the magnetic characteristics of the molecule or the magnet. By magnetic attraction atoms unite to form molecules, and molecules unite to form bodies.

And then we note electrical polarity, which is similar to that of magnetism. Any appliance for generating electricity has two opposite poles or electrodes. At one electrode the current is generated and, passing in a circuit, returns to the opposite electrode.

Now let us turn to organic nature for further evidence. Here we find the principle of propagation to depend upon what are termed the two opposite sexes —male and female. This order is maintained in the animal kingdom, and there is little doubt that, although not so apparent, the order of male and female holds throughout the vegetable kingdom. Among many plants it is known to obtain, and the scientific inference forces the conclusion that there is no break in the order of male and female in all animate nature.

In the realm of mind and the conditions of nature, which form the counterpart, we note the characteristics of good and evil, vice and virtue, love and hatred, and so on through the long list, that might be indefinitely extended. There are two opposites throughout mind, matter and force. These we call the two extremes. There is a literal up and down with reference to the earth's surface, high and low potential with reference to electricity, and corresponding to this there are "the ups and downs of life," high and low minds, etc. There are also "two sides to every question," except "the silver question," which is shown by this little book to be all on the side of bimetallism.

I leave the reader to formulate the catalogue embracing all terms which designate the conditions that properly come under the head of the two opposites, and pass on to the consideration of the conditions of animal locomotion.

While all animals are not bipeds, there is no animal that is a monoped. Quadrupeds have two pairs of legs, and the "thousand-leg" has his legs attached in pairs of twos; but a one-legged animal is an unheard-of thing. Monometallism is a financial system with one leg. I liken it to a man with one leg amputated hobbling about on the other, endeavoring to do the work of a man with two sound legs. One is as unnatural and impossible as the other. The success of monometallism, no matter what the standard, is a natural impossibility.

Again, vehicles of every description that can be operated successfully have wheels by twos. Beginning with the bicycle, we have the four-wheel buggy, carriage, and wagon, and the six- and eight-wheel locomotive. The unicycle has been invented, and serves the purpose of a vehicle about as perfectly as a single standard fills the natural requirements of a circulating currency. Everything in nature or mechanics designed to move successfully must have more than one point of support. The tricycle has three wheels and for this reason is not a popular vehicle. A body with one, three, or five movable points of support is a mechanical possibility, just as a single, triple, or quintuple standard is a financial possibility; but all alike must be unsuccessful because the principle is not in accord with natural law. A movable body, animal or mechanical, to move with the most perfect balance and least friction, must have points of support by twos. The circulating currency taken as a whole is a movable body, and to maintain a just balance and move with the least friction must have at least two points of support in the business circuit—one at the (producing) points where wealth is generated, the other at the great manufacturing and financial centers. (See Explanation of Fig. 2.)

There is no such thing as a magnet with a single pole. Break it up and each of the pieces will have two opposite poles. Break a molecule up into atoms and each atom will have opposite poles. In everything else nature endeavors to maintain normal conditions. She is endeavoring to teach man by the penalty of her laws the right way to live. Every punishment she inflicts is evidently intended for a lesson in natural law. We blame nature for many things when the blame should fall on ourselves. We are continually warned, but we are slow to heed.

The reason we are slow to heed is not so much the result of our ignorance of natural laws and their penalties as that our propensities, lusts, appetites, and passions stand in our way. Nature teaches millions of object-lessons in temperance by the terrible penalties she inflicts on the intemperate, and yet the appetite or the groveling lust for pleasure blinds millions more to their fate, and down they go under the penalty of natural law.

And so men are blinded by their lust for gold until, mad with the pitiless passion, they violate the laws of their own being, outrage the rights and liberties of others, and finally die, it may be, cursing God. In spite of all the sad lessons that nature has taught mankind for indulging their lust for gold, men will still make gold their god and defy nature to do her worst. Nations have fallen before the fierce ravages of greed because, in the madness of passion, men violated natural laws which govern human rights and liberties.

Be not deceived; nature has moral as well as mechanical laws. Every natural law governing human life and action is a moral law. The letter of these laws means strict morality; character and purity are given to those who implicitly obey them.

But there is no escaping the penalties for violations of natural law. Wealth confers no special privileges under these laws. Multimillionaires may bribe legislatures, courts, and juries, intimidate and oppress the poor for a season, but they will find that nature has no more regard for them than she has for a tramp. She is, indeed, no respecter of persons. Instead of the penalty of exposure, cold, and hunger she inflicts on the tramp for improvidence, she places in the rich man's closet a grim-visaged skeleton to continually remind him that life to him is a disappointment and a mistake. He drinks the sweets from the cup that wealth places in his hand, and nature will not permit him to remove it from his lips until he drinks the dregs, which turn to gall at the last.

The single gold standard, which is the legitimate offspring of lust for gold, is cursing this land with poverty, wretchedness, and dishonesty; but I warn the perpetrators of the infamous crime that nature holds them accountable and will vindicate her laws. If you pull down the pillars of state, the tumbling walls will crush you with the rest. My hope is that your political locks will be shorn by the voters of the country in 1900, and that they will forever after have the good sense to prevent their growth again.

In this little and somewhat hastily written treatise I have endeavored to prove that the reforms demanded by the reform element of the country are thoroughly in accord with natural law. Drummond's "Natural Law in the Spiritual World" was considered an innovation on old-established lines of religious thought, but the author might well have broadened his title and discourse to have covered all the conditions of nature up to nature's God. The jurisdiction of natural law is unlimited. Man with all his institutions is as much under the direction of

Natural laws the true model for human laws.

natural law as are the plants and animals below him. Human institutions, if rightly framed, are copied from counterpart institutions of nature. Man has instituted a circular system of business and finance. The purpose of this system is to so regulate business, trade, and finance that they will work together freely and interchangeably, maintaining a just equilibrium at every point of the circuit. Now money, consisting of gold and silver in certain measurable quantities and fixed as the standard of values, should freely circulate from hand to hand in exchange for commodities and articles of use.

The counterpart in nature is her vast system of circulation, in which there is no break or flaw. It is by this system that a just equilibrium of matter and of force is maintained. From this system all change is evolved. The circularity in the motions of the earth on its axis and around the sun causes the circularity of time measured by days and nights and the seasons. From the alternations of days and nights and the seasons all change is evolved, which, taking the form and nature of its cause, is circular in all its countless evolutions. (See Fig. 1.)

Nature is truth and all her parts are truths. Nature has no straight lines; she is a system of curves, circuits, cycles, and evolutions. A straight line is the line of error in thinking and reasoning—a tangent of a circuit of truth. The single gold standard may therefore be defined as a tangent of the circuit of business.

In his system of finance man established a ratio of

values of gold and silver, and that ratio was copied from the balance-sheet of the relative production of the two metals, which indicated that nature had stored about sixteen ounces of silver to one of gold. The commercial use of the metals when on an honest basis of free circulation has proved that the ratio fixed by nature should be maintained. True, the relative quantities in the production of the two metals have varied at different times, but these fluctuations were due to sudden rich discoveries of one or the other of the metals, or to unjust discriminations in favor of one as against the other. There is no question but that nature has, in the relative quantities she has stored in the earth, fixed the normal and just commercial ratio of the precious metals.

This must be true. She has fixed the ratio of other metals in the relative quantities she deposited in the rocks, which has been found to be the ratio of mechanical requirements. Of all the deposits of minerals coal is the most abundant. Unlike iron, lead, copper, etc., coal is consumed in its use, and its extensive use tends to exhaust the supply more rapidly than does the use of all the metals combined.

Nature has made free and abundant provisions for all the needs and requirements of mankind, and she has instituted over all wise laws, which, if observed, would develop a civilization beside which our own would appear, as it really is, a refined barbarism characterized by ingenious crimes and cruelties. The laws of such a civilization would necessarily conform to natural laws. Nature is systematic in all her laws and conditions, all her parts working together to secure the perfect harmony of the whole. The laws of such a civilization would duplicate that system which would secure national and international harmony. The intelligent principle rules in nature and so in a perfect human government. I would describe such a civilization as one governed by a few simple and fixed laws, with the certain infliction of penalties for all violations. Nature has but a few fixed laws, but they are so ordered as to provide for the working out of all the details of her vast system. Let us instance the law of attraction. Wherever there is matter, from atom to planet and from planet to systems of planets, the law of attraction is in operation.

In a human government one law would not properly restrain greed, which, under our present financial system, should be the fundamental purpose of laws. I can see the necessity for the enactment of three laws, viz.: first, free international commerce, or free trade; second, absolutely prohibit individual or corporate speculations in the necessaries and comforts of life; third, remove the cause and forever prohibit drunkenness. Such laws would make of this nation one of prosperous homes and a temperate people. They would cover the contingencies of all time, because they would shut up the fountain of the great evils that afflict society and government. All lesser evils spring from the sources which would be suppressed by the three laws named. "Man's in-

[margin: Three laws for restraint of greed.]

humanity to man" is wholly the fault of defective laws and institutions of government. To remedy these defects is the solemn duty of this civilization.

The world has never produced a class of men equal to the task. Our forefathers founded a republic with laws adequate for the time, but subsequent history shows their sad lack of foresight. Besides planting the war germ of slavery on our shores, they made no legal provision whatever for the control of greed. They had read history back to Moses, but in the time of victory for human liberty they seemed to forget that under no form of government could greed so flourish as under one of free institutions. The evils of Europe were introduced, fostered, and grew with the growth of the republic. The mistaken notion that individual liberty was more sacred than the welfare of the public became a deep-rooted and dangerous theory, which to-day lies at the bottom of all objection to legal interference with prevailing evils.

But the task of freeing men from the grasp of greed is ours. No matter whom or how we blame, we face the living monster, greed, that has fattened upon the toil, gloried in the shrieks and moans of the downtrodden and oppressed, until he is mad with power. He now challenges—he soon will defy—interference. The question is, my fellow-voter, shall we submit? Will we submit and be dragged down to a servitude that is more galling, more beastly, more heartless than slavery? Do I believe it? Do you believe it? Yes; every intelligent voter in this land knows that these words are true. What, then, hinders the needed reforms? We all hope, and some of us even dare to believe, that they will come. We all long for relief from the body of this social and political death. We are weary of this unequal struggle, this godless, heartless scramble for—what? Some for wealth, and others, the vast majority, for bare subsistence. Oh, the ceaseless round of drudge and drudge, with scarce a moment's respite from miserable, debasing drudgery! Turn where we will, it is drudgery: the rich man drudging his life out over his arduous, never-ending task as he bends wearily under the load that none but the rich know how to bear; the struggling aspirant for wealth, who is bending every energy and sacrificing every spark of manhood to attain it; the poor, on the farm, in the store or shop, toiling on, worn out, discouraged, and smarting under the lash of injustice; the poor indeed, the toilers, employed and unemployed, a great army that is crowding and clamoring for bare subsistence—all, all lead a life of drudgery, all but the indolent offspring of the rich.

Yes; millions there are in the United States whose souls have long since been offered up on the altar of crushed and ruined hopes and blighted lives. The struggling legions of the homeless, helpless, and dependent; the thousands of haggard and hungry tenement-dwellers and outcasts on the streets; the scores of thousands whose avocations are recounted only by the catalogue of crime; the swarms of human parasites, from the exceedingly minute ones, who subsist upon the weakness and depravity of their fellow-creatures, to the great ones, who prey upon all classes and conditions—these, I say, form a great part of our population, and these never feel the warm glow of a patriotic impulse.

Oh, the desperate, heartless struggle for wealth where there is the shadow of a chance to attain it, the bitter, galling struggle for subsistence where poverty has set its dismal seal, and the woeful blood-curdling struggle for things under the protection of human laws by those whose lives are branded by the curse of crime! How awful the picture! Cities reeking with poverty and the rottenness of evils and crime, villages and towns diseased to the very core by the blighting touch of greed, and the whole country staggering under her load of wealth, poverty, wretchedness, and rottenness.

Problems? The future of our country presents nothing but problems. The government of the United States is a national experiment, the grandest ever known on earth. *An appeal for patriotism.* We are approaching the crisis when the success or failure of the experiment shall be known —when it will be determined whether or not the people are capable of self-government. I have had great confidence in the stability of our free institutions, but I confess that that confidence is waning. I greatly fear that national dissolution is setting in and that the corpse will soon be ready for burial. I am sure that if constitutional remedies are not soon administered the world will be called upon to perform the funeral rites over the remains of a once glorious nation, that died from a complication of the diseases of greed, hoarded wealth, poverty, evils, and crime.

The question is, who is to blame? The round of abuses seems to be continuous, and when you touch one you touch all. The first cause is greed; then follow hoarded wealth, poverty, evils, and crime; and by repeating hoarded wealth comes next, which, in the order of succession, shows that crime lies very close to hoarded wealth and hoarded wealth to crime. Hoarded wealth, poverty, evils, crime, hoarded wealth, etc. Poverty on one side of hoarded wealth, crime on the other, and evils between poverty and crime. Take your pencil and draw a circle, then write the words around it in the order given above, the word "greed" being written at the center, and you will see the exact relation of the words to one another as applied to the political, financial, and social condition of our country.

It is a hard picture, but let me tell you, in all candor, it is drawn true to life. I have no interest in saying so if it were not so. But do you say that hoarded wealth is responsible for all the poverty, evils, and crime in the land? I answer without the slightest hesitation that it is practically responsible for their abnormal development, and the national government primarily responsible for its creation. By legislation evils have been fostered which are formidable allies of plutocrats in that they impoverish multitudes annually and fit them for the labor market, which, being overstocked, reduces the compensation for labor proportionally to the number of impoverished and dependent victims.

As wealth accumulates in the hands of the few, the people become more grasping and corrupt, the weak go to the wall of poverty, multitudes drop through the pitfalls of evils, and hosts become criminals in the corrupt and unequal struggle for spoils. This is a palpable truth, and the singular thing is that the few who control the greater part of the wealth of the United States do not see it. Why they do not see in the signs of the times ominous forebodings of popular discontent, the increasing labor leagues with their increasing numbers, and the destroying angel of anarchism with the resistless weapon of dynamite, is a great mystery. They know little of human nature if they take no warning from popular discontent, organized labor, anarchism, and dynamite.

You say this is harsh talk. It is, but it comes from a patriotic and philanthropic heart. I can say with the poet, "This is my own, my native land." I have an interest in the perpetuity of our free institutions that is interwoven with my heartstrings. I can stand in the brunt of the battle and bear the harsher tread of the iron heel for the sake of peace, but there are those who will survive me, whose budding lives will blossom into youth and ripen into manhood, and whose future is as tendrils twining around every aspiration and hope I cherish. How it would grieve me if I knew their tender feet must tread a thorny path, and then, at life's high noontide, look through tears of anguish from crushed and hopeless poverty to life's setting sun, whose last rays, perchance, may fall upon shackles and chains!

Yes; I feel an interest in my country's welfare deeper than all the hoarded millions of earth could give, because I love our erring country, our liberties, and, it may be most of all, the little lives that some day will be without my protecting arm, my sympathy, my love, but must fight life's battles single-handed and alone. For the sake of these dear ties and the benediction of a duty well and faithfully performed, I strive with pen and tongue to have men—all men —think, that they may act wisely, nobly, and honestly in their relations to country, posterity, and their own best interests.

I long with millions more for better times, but let us not be deceived by any one into believing that they will come about naturally. It *A talk with voters.* is to the interest of bondholders, stock-jobbers, and market manipulators to make us believe that they hold the destiny of this nation in their own hands, and that if they have "confidence" they will invest their capital, which would make times good. Do not let them scare you with that word "confidence." It is a scarecrow to intimidate you, so that you will say nothing against capital, nor vote against its interest. It ought to be perfectly clear to every intelligent voter that if the people let capital have its way it will surely enslave them.

And do not labor under the delusion that all the reforms spoken of in this little book can be brought about at a single stroke. Remember, reforms move slowly. A perfect government is certainly desirable, but we must remember that much of our voting strength is raw mat rial and will have to pass through a long educational process before it can be relied upon to vote right. I have touched upon about all the prevalent social and political evils, but this was necessary in following out the trend of natural laws. Nature is opposed to all evils, individual, social, and political. The evils that should engage the immediate attention of voters, however, are trusts, market manipulations, and the single gold standard. It is more important that we have a free market and free circulation of money than free coinage of silver. If we have a free market and free circulation of money we can get along and do business with less currency. Both these reforms are necessary, however, and should be pushed vigorously until the election day of 1900.

Do not be afraid of being called an anarchist. Remember that ridicule is the weapon of a weak and dishonest cause. In the late campaign every man who stood squarely opposed to trusts and the gold conspiracy was called an anarchist and repudiator. This is because the advocates of trusts and the single gold standard had no argument to offer in support of the gigantic system of robbery which they were striving to fasten upon the people. They dared not come out openly in support of trusts, so these single-gold-standard advocates made a great outcry against the restoration of silver to its proper place with gold, and called it repudiation. The friends of free silver advocated reforms that strike directly at the vitals of plutocracy, and their opponents called them anarchists. Is it anarchy for the people—the sovereigns of this republic—to justly criticize their public servants? Is it anarchy for the people to criticize the unjust ruling of the Supreme Court in the income-tax case, or to denounce unwarranted federal interference which was in violation of law? Is the Supreme Court or the President or any public servant above the reach of popular criticism? Is the servant above his master? Our Declaration of Independence says that this government derives its just powers from the consent of the governed. According to this, every official in the United States derives all official authority from the people. Do the people grant to the Supreme Court the right to decide that the rich shall not pay a just proportion of expenses of the government? If not, is it anarchistic for the people to object to such a ruling? Are all the millions of people who indorsed the Chicago platform by voting for Mr. Bryan anarchists? Were all the representative men who composed the Chicago convention and formulated the platform anarchists? Is Senator Teller, who walked out of the Republican convention at St. Louis because he could no longer stand with a party that would fasten upon the people the single gold standard, with all the injustice that such a conspiracy will breed, an anarchist?

Who are the real anarchists, anyway? Herr Most and his followers are avowed anarchists, and during the late campaign Herr Most was openly in favor of the single gold standard.

What is the great cause of anarchy? It is the unequal distribution of wealth and the abuse of the power it gives to the few who acquire an unjust proportion. Are men anarchists who favor lawful measures for the restraint of the cause of anarchism? Yet these are the kind of men the single-gold-standard advocates brand as anarchists. Indeed, they brand every advocate of political reforms as an anarchist. Most of them are paid for their services by great reform-wreckers, who are also fortune-wreckers, home-wreckers, and life-wreckers. Pay no attention to their ridicule. As you stand for reform, be sure you favor none but just means for attaining it, and no matter how you are accused, you will know that you are not only opposed to anarchy, but to anarchy-breeding as well.

Let us stick to silver and gold, as not only the money of the Constitution, but as the money of nature as well. Tell the opponents of silver that in the support of bimetallism you have the unanswerable argument of nature in the philosophy of her laws and conditions, and the logic of all history of the use of metals, to sustain you. Tell them that, because you are opposed to the demonetization of silver, you are therefore opposed to repudiation. Demonetization of silver is the worst form of repudiation, since it repudiates the money of the Constitution and of nature. If they dare to say "53-cent dollar," ask them what the price of a silver dollar was prior to 1873, and what happened at that date to reduce the price. Ask them if it is not true that all the prestige and power of Cleveland's last administration was used to degrade the value of silver.

And this is a severely practical question: If the single gold standard will bring permanent prosperity to all the people and to the government, how comes it that from 1893, the date of the repeal of the Sherman Act, to 1896, both inclusive, the country experienced the most disastrous panic known to its history, and the government (the people) was burdened by a vast bonded indebtedness? If, in reply, they claim that capitalists were intimidated by the free-silver movement and withheld their money from investments, which precipitated the panic, ask them if that is not pretty strong evidence that capitalists have a corner on money. In fact, the evidence is conclusive. Look at it. By simply withholding their money from circulation capitalists can precipitate a disastrous panic! Disastrous to whom? To capitalists? Go and ask the farmer, the small business man, the laboring classes. They will point you to their wrecked homes and business, to a host of half-paid, overworked employés, and to a vast army of men and women in enforced idleness. Are capitalists benefited by such a condition? Why not? It hastens the consummation of their desire to control the wealth of the nation. Continued long enough, the desire would be consummated. Having practical control of the money of the country, it is but a step to controlling its wealth. That step is easy—simply withhold the money from circulation. Here is authority for this statement:

"Fifty men in these United States have it in their power, by reason of the wealth they control, to come together within the next twenty-four hours and arrive at an understanding by which every wheel of trade and commerce may be stopped from revolving, every avenue of trade blocked, and every electric key struck dumb. These fifty men can paralyze the whole country, for they control the circulation of the currency and can create a panic whenever they will."*

Mr. Depew, being one of the fifty men, knew what he was talking about. And right here is the "niggah in de wood-pile." With the free and unlimited coinage of silver fifty men could not "control the circulation of the currency," and this would break up the great conspiracy to control the wealth of the nation. Capitalists would then find it impossible to precipitate a panic by withholding their gold from circulation. The business of the country can be conducted with silver (or silver certificates) in such an emergency, and no one knows it better than the capitalists.

Every other trust is subordinate to the money trust, which may be defined as the single gold standard. So long as that trust is legally secure, so long will all anti-trust laws be inoperative. I say inoperative, because I am not foolish enough to believe that our representatives who are pledged to perpetuate the money trust (the single gold standard) would break faith with their constituents, to whom they owe their election.

* Chauncey Depew, in 1893.

But we are now promised a return of prosperity to the whole country. Glowing accounts are published in the newspapers of the revival of business and the active investment of capital. Thousands of idle men are reported to have been given employment and everywhere the wheels of industry given increased momentum. Many people look upon these reports as the harbingers of permanent prosperity.

Be not deceived. Permanent prosperity cannot be brought about by artificial means. Capital may intoxicate business and trade by the stimulant of increased employment of labor in factories and shops, large loans of money on farms, and by spasmodic investments; but when it is found that the producing classes of the country are too poor to purchase the goods and material of the factories and shops, and that capitalists have been trading jack-knives with one another, then will business and trade "sober up" and find their condition worse than when they were put under the influence of the stimulant. The statement that the permanent prosperity of the country is entirely dependent upon the prosperity of the producing classes cannot be too often repeated. It is a statement of fact that everybody should understand, and none so thoroughly as the laboring classes.

Beware of political deceptions.

We cannot grow rich trading jack-knives. Wealth must be first produced before it can be had. Money is not wealth. The victory of "sound (?) money" has "restored confidence," they say, and now there is money to loan at very low rates of interest. Well, suppose $500,000,000 are loaned and borrowed on the strength of the victory. Why, $500,000,000 of debt is saddled upon the people who have borrowed it, secured in greater part by mortgages on homes. Mortgages are the seeds of land monopoly, and land monopoly is the curse of any nation afflicted by it. The $500,000,000 goes into circulation, you say? Yes; but in time it goes out of circulation through the manipulations of trusts and other moneyed concerns. And so the moneyed classes loan the money and get it back, together with the land, when the mortgages are foreclosed. Start up the factories, all of them, in full blast, and how long will they run without purchasers? And how can there be purchasers when there is not money enough in circulation to transact the regular business and trade of the country?

Abolish trusts and put more money into circulation by the free and unlimited coinage of gold and silver, and then the people will cause the earth to produce wealth, and there will be active money enough to establish a normal circuit of business and trade, through which products would pass to the consumers, and just equivalents in money flow back by return circuit to the producers. (See Fig. 2.) This is nature's method for restoring real prosperity to the country. There is no other method or device worth considering. Mark that!

Of all that is said and written of the effects of prevalent evils, we hear and read little of the worst and most threatening to the stability of our free institutions. All interest seems to concentrate on the financial effects, which are noted as business failures, bankruptcy, and the increasing poverty of the many in contrast with the increasing wealth and aristocratic tendencies of the few. These unequal conditions are considered dangerous only in so far as they tend to undermine the liberties of the many and reduce them to a state of servitude to the few.

<small>*Demoralizing effects of political evils.*</small>

In seeking out the causes, little attention is paid to the first great cause of the evil, which I wish to point out and discuss. That cause consists in the generally demoralizing effect which the unscrupulous business methods of the few have upon the public mind, backed and encouraged as they are by the executive, judicial, and legislative branches of the government. The effect of all this is the prevalent tendency among the people to copy the examples set by men in high places. People are prone to take the rich and powerful, or those who lead in the councils of the nation, as models, and to justify their own personal acts on the ground that their superiors set the example.

And right here is the true beginning of national disintegration. No argument is needed to reinforce the fact that morality is the corner-stone and the foundation of all good government and society. When that corner-stone and foundation begin to crumble away, the loftier and more massive the superstructure of government and society, the more eminent the peril and destructive the effects of the fall.

It has been so ordered in the very constitution of nature that man, the only element of her vast mechanism that has the capacity to reason and the ability to choose, shall learn wisdom of her laws and choose obedience to them as the true guide of all his ways. However much he may ignore moral laws as nonessential to his prosperity, he will find, as he ever has found, that behind them is the stern executor ready to inflict the sure penalty for every violation. True moral law is natural law and cannot be violated with impunity. In individual cases the infliction of the penalty may not always be apparent to the superficial observer, who cannot see beyond the pomp and splendor that blind him.

But there are those who stand too near the hearth and home of the rich and great to be affected by the optical illusion, which is but the creation of vanity in the mind of the far-off observer. Around the cold, proud hearth and home the wise student of human life sees no light, not even of joy or peace. Looking into the gilded palace of the king, he notes the fear and trembling of the tyrant ruler and sadly says, " Uneasy rests the head that wears the crown." Vainly he seeks to find happiness where sincerity, friendship, and a lofty regard for the rights of others have no abiding-place. He knows that wealth, learning, and the authority of office cannot take the place of these divinely human attributes.

So a nation whose people grow deceptive, unfriendly, and immorally selfish is not only driving prosperity from its homes, but happiness as well. The people of such a nation cannot long be prosperous, and never happy; nay, not even intellectual in the loftier and nobler sense. Selfish, grasping greed cannot be truly moral or intellectual. Let a Washington or a Webster be consumed by debasing lust for gold, and their great powers of mind would ultimately shrink to counterfeit statesmanship and broad cunning, such as characterizes much of what now passes for statesmanship.

Let the ear be struck dumb to nature's heart-throbs and the eye be blinded to her grandeur by the hand of greed, and poetry and song are hushed, joys that swell the human heart to lofty raptures are flown, and science becomes the perverted slave of base and hopeless materialism.

And so statesmanship, poetry, song, and science too, as man once revered it as "a psalm and a prayer," are fast dying in this land. The prophets, poets, and sages of old looked aloft when they communed with nature in prophecy, in song, in the wisdom and eloquence of tongue and pen. Now we go with our faces to the dust, looking for cold, hard gold, as cold and hard as our hearts. We look down for gold, for all things we call wealth, and, thinking of nothing else, we follow the trend of our sight and thoughts and go down, down to selfishness and the practice of mean deceptions, down to a low contempt for the rights of others, down to polite dishonesty and refined barbarism.

The cry goes up from all over the land, Where are our poets? Where are our philosophers? Where are our statesmen? I ask, How can a poet sing when all about him is discord and maddening strife? How can a philosopher be known when there are none to understand? How can a statesman lead the people out into the open light of liberty when all the hosts of greed unite to oppose and defeat him?

And literature? It has been more than a generation since the decline in literature began. That marks the period of the general decline of moral and intellectual greatness. We have few great writers, because there are few great readers. Men have little leisure to read or think. The world is all too busy now for great writers, readers, or thinkers. The craze for accumulating wealth and the problem of bread and butter concern men more than high-born literature. Genius and great talents are bought and sold like so much merchandise. Everything must have a commercial value to have any value at all. A great discovery in science or invention is counted worthless unless it can be put on the market and sold.

The greatest thing of the hour is the "almighty dollar." To get it men will scheme, cheat, and lie. These are the elements of our latest business methods. Wherever these methods are successfully employed it is called "business." In money-getting the end justifies the means, no matter how dishonest or inhuman the means to be employed. In much of the business dealings of the country neither fairness nor mercy are shown or expected. Most men are coming to believe that no man living is unselfishly honest. Suspicion is everywhere. If you point them to a man who, they are persuaded, is honest, they tell you he is a "crank." This would be said of a man who would copy even the example of Socrates, to say nothing of that example which millions profess to be following—most of them, I fear, afar off.

It is not doubted that people were once honest, but it no longer "pays," so they say it has been abandoned. "It doesn't pay." "There is no money in it." "There is no longer any room in the world for an honest man," for they say unselfish honesty means poverty and starvation.

Where there is no unselfish honesty there is no sincerity or friendship and no lofty regard for the rights of others. Where these are not, the seeds of anarchy are already sown. The great truth that "whatsoever a man soweth, that shall he also reap," is as applicable to society and government as to an individual member. Unless these seeds are destroyed we will ultimately reap anarchy and national ruin. This was the harvest of ancient Greece and Rome, and this will be the harvest of all nations for all time that, by first sowing seeds of political deception and dishonesty, encourage the people to sow broadcast the seeds of national disruption and ruin.

The first seeds of anarchy that were sown in this country were in the form of political deceptions practised upon the people. It began long ago, but was checked from time to time by great statesmen like Clay, Webster, Jackson, and other copatriots. Finally the Civil War came and left its blight in the institution of a party that inaugurated a system of class legislation, which resulted in the formation of powerful corporations, trusts, syndicates, and combines, which are now plundering the wealth of the people.

First seeds of anarchy.

It is needless to say that these institutions are the legitimate fruits of the high protective tariff. Under it our government has been one of paternalism to moneyed interests. While colossal fortunes were piling up for the manipulators of protected industries and articles of manufacture, labor was forced to organize against the unjust exactions of the tariff-favored employers. Still, labor voted for it because political leaders deceived it by the delusive campaign shout of "Protection to American labor!" Many producers voted for it because in the next breath these demagogues would shout, "Protection to American products!" Many a deluded business man voted for it because he was made to believe that his business depended upon "Protection to American industries!"

Meantime people of all classes paid as cost price on nearly all goods and articles they purchased the exorbitant tariff added to the first cost of manufacture, the profits on the labor employed in the factories, and the added profits of middlemen. And the beauty of the great deception lies in the fact that the highest tariff was laid on the necessaries and comforts of life, while luxuries, such as none but the rich can buy, were almost exempt from the tariff tax. As a result of the tremendous profits derived from the tariff tax, protected interests were enabled to hoard vast sums of money, which has given them the control of the circulating currency, the markets, legislation, and finally the whole machinery of government.

To accomplish all this, the powerful trusts that the high protective tariff created have resorted to bribery, trickery, and fraud to secure further legislation favorable to their own interests. Emboldened by their success, they advanced a step further and secured the favorable ruling of the courts and finally the Supreme Court. Thus many of the political leaders of the country were corrupted and their usefulness forever destroyed.

Out of it all, complications arose, in the midst of which nearly all the leaders of the two old parties stood side by side. There was no longer an issue to separate them. It had been a fight for spoils, and there were no spoils for either side to champion the rights and interests of the people. So they joined hands, formed the great party of plutocracy, and defeated the party of the people by methods and means which, if ever fully known and written, will form the darkest page in American history.

Who wonders that corruption is abroad in the land? I wonder that the people are not even more corrupt and less intellectual than they are.

FREE TRADE

I HAVE endeavored to show in the preceding pages of this little book that before the birth of the race nature provided for the needs and wants of the human family for all time. This was done during the geological periods, when the crude material for soil was formed from the debris of the rocks, ground away by the action of the waters of the earth, lashed into fury by storm and tempest through the successive ages of disturbances. This debris was made into crude soil by chemical action, which first formed mold, then vegetation; and after countless ages of decaying vegetation the soil, deep and productive, was evolved. During the periods of geological disturbances the mountains were thrown up by the action of subterranean forces, inundating vast forests, which by chemical change were formed into coal-beds. In the fissures of the strata of rock that formed the mountain-ranges nature deposited the metals—silver, gold, iron, copper, lead, and so on through the list—in quantities of each kind proportionally to meet the requirements of the human family during its race-life.

From the soil and the mines come all things we call wealth: from the soil all food and clothing, from the mines coal and all the metals. Taking a glance over the earth's surface, we see that nature has fashioned continents and islands for the habitation of man. Of them all, we note that the American continent leads in the vastness of resources—a continent capable of producing sufficient raw materials to feed and clothe the world. We note that it has the newest civilization and that its resources are only partially developed.

Crossing the waters, we find the old civilization of Europe with a population crowding upon her depleting resources. Her vast population must be fed and clothed, so great manufacturing industries have been founded for the purpose of converting the raw materials of the soil into food and clothing. Portions of Europe are almost exclusively devoted to manufacturing. Cheap labor, which is the natural result of her crowding population, cheapens the cost of goods from her factories to a point that almost precludes competition.

Necessarily, then, England is a typical manufacturing country. Her people must be fed and clothed, and this the resources of the country will not do. The raw materials must be purchased of producing nations, and her people must earn them by toil. In no way can they be employed except in manufactories. Her limited territory and dense population compel this condition.

On the other hand, the United States is a country

of practically inexhaustible resources, which are in the early infancy of development, and thinly populated compared with any of the old countries. This is indeed a new country, with its destiny in the hands of its people, and upon the wisdom of their laws depends the greatness of that destiny. It is a nation where liberty is enthroned and where the people by the ballot wield the scepter of power.

The people have ever been, and still are, ambitious to make this the greatest nation on the face of the globe. They have consented to legislation which they believed would be conducive to that end. In their pardonable desire to add to the greatness of our resources the greatness of a matchless civilization, they thoughtlessly adopted at least two measures of whose results, if they had been more wise and less enthusiastic, they would have foreseen the danger. Briefly, these measures were the protective tariff and unrestricted foreign immigration.

The first of these measures was enacted into law; the other is a time-honored unwritten law. They are both force measures intended to compel the rapid growth and settlement of the country. In the exuberance of our national youth we were impatient for rapid growth; populating the country by natural increase and restricted immigration was too slow. We had great resources and we needed a great population to develop them, was the logic of our impatience.

It was apparent, too, that with our fabulous resources we could be commercially independent and self-sustaining. Accordingly, it was decided that this should be a manufacturing as well as a producing country. This it could not be and compete with foreign manufactories. So tariff laws were enacted by which a tax was levied on foreign goods, the revenue accruing therefrom to be used for defraying the expenses of the government.

With the accession of the Republican party to the control of the government, this tax on foreign imports became practically prohibitory. It was termed the "high protective tariff," and is briefly discussed elsewhere in this book.

My object now is to prove that both the unwritten law of unrestricted foreign immigration and the "protective tariff" conflict with wise national economy. To do this it is necessary to go back to first principles—nature—and get our bearings.

At the outset I ask, What is the basis of the broadest national prosperity? Answer: A nation made up largely of producing classes, who find a ready sale for their products at a profit, is the most independent as well as prosperous. No man is so independent as the prosperous producer, and no nation is so independent and prosperous as one of prosperous producing classes. On the other hand, no nation is so weak and powerless as one made up of nonproducing and consequently homeless classes. This is perfectly natural. Cut off from access to the soil and without means, a man is in dependent circumstances. A nation made up largely of such men is in dependent circumstances.

Witness the condition of England. If her people were commercially cut off from all producing nations, the large majority of them would starve to death in a very short time. The people of the United States or any other producing nation can live indefinitely without international commerce. Our people produce and manufacture much more than they eat and wear, and would finally produce one hundredfold more if there were more legislation in the interest of the producing classes and less to subsidize manufactories and trusts.

If it is clearly true that a nation of products, producers, and homes is more prosperous and independent than any other, then it necessarily follows that in a nation of resources all legislation should be directed toward that very desirable end. This being true, is it not equally true that the protective tariff defeats this very end? In fact, does not all tariff legislation arise from a false theory of national economics? Let us see.

Suppose a policy of free trade had been adopted at the close of the Revolution and adhered to up to the present time; what do you say, reader, would have been the condition of this country compared with what it is? There is but one intelligent answer to that question, viz.: We would have fewer factories and a vastly greater number of farms, fewer non-producers and homeless, and a greater number of producers and homes. Europe would have been our market for our products and raw materials. In turn we would have been a purchaser of her manufactured goods. Thus our farming industries would have been stimulated by the increased purchases of Europe, and our people would have saved the millions of dollars annually that they paid out as tariff on home-manufactured goods.

As trusts and combines generally are the legitimate outgrowth of the tariff system, so the vast sums of money hoarded in our great banking institutions represent, directly or indirectly, profits resulting from the tariff tax. If, under a free-trade system, the balance of trade were in favor of Europe, it would aggregate but a small sum compared with the amount of money derived from the tariff and now out of circulation. And it matters little to the people where money is hoarded, whether in banks and vaults on Wall Street or those on Lombard Street. If there be a difference, it is in favor of Lombard Street, as in that event the money would hardly be used here as a political corruption fund.

With free trade we would now have no trusts, syndicates, or combines controlling the markets and sapping the wealth of the people. There would be little monopoly of land, as every acre of tillable land in the country would be under cultivation, yielding crops at a fair profit to owners. Our cities would not be so large and there would be fewer towns, because there would not be so many non-producers; but their people would be better paid, fed, and clothed, because they would not be overpopulated as they are to-day.

Along with free trade there should have been a

restrictive immigration law, prohibiting the landing of paupers, dangerous classes, and families with less than five hundred dollars. Much more under our tariff system has such a law been needed. Our labor is entitled to protection from pauper labor, and our people and free institutions from the danger of trusting hordes of illiterate and irresponsible foreigners with the ballot.*

But what does nature say for free trade? Listen! She has a broader and a loftier patriotism than has man. Man provides for his family and his kind, but nature provides for all her children, and, like a wise parent, saves the best for the last. In the natural course of events the eastern hemisphere was populated first and the western hemisphere last. The eastern needed the western hemisphere, and it was discovered. The resources of the New World were needed with which to feed and clothe the crowding population of the Old World. Civilization needed room in which to expand. As evidently decreed before the world was that the whole earth should be in-

---

* The following statistics, copied from the New York "World," show to what extent Europe has availed itself of the opportunity afforded by the unreasonable leniency of our immigration laws. It will be seen incidentally that the States named in the following list gave Mr. McKinley large majorities, which shows that his election was due to the foreign vote. These are the States, with their percentage of foreign population: Massachusetts, 56 per cent.; Rhode Island, 59; New York, 57; Pennsylvania, 37; Ohio, 35; Iowa, 44; Illinois, 50; Michigan, 55; South Dakota, 61; Wisconsin, 74; Minnesota, 76; North Dakota, 79.

habited by the human race, civilized and enlightened, so we find here in the western hemisphere, in the overflow, the promise of the early fulfilment of the decree.

Behind the actions of every sane man are purposes, though often misguided. Behind nature are purposes infinitely wise and absolutely infallible. These purposes are enacted into natural laws which are supreme over all. They are the great Magna Charta and constitution for the proper government of the race, perfect in minutest detail, applying alike and impartially to each and every individual of the countless generations of men. If we interpret natural laws as they apply to national life without regard to the well-being of the race-life, we evidently err. International commerce and social relationship forbid it. We should approve the wisest methods for the ushering in of that golden age, "the brotherhood of man."

With the international commercial and social relations that now exist, one civilized nation cannot rise high in the line of true advancement independent of the others. Through these international connections passes interchangeably the invisible spirit of the laws and institutions of each and all the nations, acting as an equalizer and tending to reduce them all to a common level. This is the result of natural law. We as a nation have been touched by the influence of English institutions and customs, and we are establishing an aristocracy of wealth that fain would duplicate in this land the old institutions of English royalty and nobility.

Catching the spirit of our free institutions when

the early patriots stamped them with that nobility of character which, in contrast, cheapened and made mean the empty honors of lordly titles, English institutions moved slowly toward the example of the ideal republic, and to-day the Queen is little more than a titled figurehead. All nations have moved slowly upward to catch us, and, alas! we have moved downward to meet them in their upward march.

There is individual life, national life, and the race or international life, and a principle that holds in one holds in all. A nation is an aggregation of individuals, and civilization in its broadest sense is the aggregation of individual nations. The former is a family of individuals, the latter a family of nations.

I have devoted much of this little book to the discussion of the weaknesses and wilfulness of the members of our own little national family, without regard to its membership in the great family of nations. I have tried to point the way to a higher national life by directing the individual judgment and conscience to the observance of natural law as the sure guide of all the affairs of state. It is now my task to follow the unerring trend of that law, which leads up to a loftier conception of human life.

Going back to the natural law that enjoins free circulation of currency, we find that, if we adopt that law into the business and commercial affairs of our own nation, we have no authority or precedent for drawing the line beyond which we may refuse to admit the application of the law. If

Natural law enjoins free trade.

the free, uninterrupted circulation of currency is enjoined by natural law as the true basis upon which business and trade should be conducted in this nation, then we cannot draw the line on the operation of the law between this and other nations with which we may have commercial relations. Now there cannot be free circulation of currency where there is a break in the circuit of business or commerce. The tariff is a break in the international commercial circuit that joins this with other nations. The circulation of currency is therefore restricted to the volume of business transacted.

Free trade means an unbroken international commercial circuit and consequently free circulation of currency. This is natural law. The reciprocal actions between the vegetable and animal kingdoms are free. The wants of one are supplied by the wastes of the other. Now let us apply this law to international commerce. Our surplus raw materials are in a sense the waste of our resources. Other nations want them. They will give us the equivalent in money. Shall we follow the injunction of natural law and supply their wants? England, we will say, takes our raw materials and manufactures them into goods. She has a surplus and therefore a waste. If other nations want them and will pay the equivalent in money, shall she supply their wants? Shall we violate the law by keeping our surplus materials (wastes), and out of them forcing the supply of our wants in manufactured goods at a heavy loss of national vitality by depleting our circulating currency? What would you think of a natural law that would force a tree to supply material for its growth from its own waste, or force an animal to subsist upon its own waste? This could be done only at the cost of the vitality of the tree and animal, just as the forced operation of the protective tariff is at the cost of the depletion of the circulating currency and the consequent loss of national vitality.

It is evident that the protective tariff is a force measure, clearly in opposition to natural law, injurious in its effects, and therefore wrong. So very injurious are its effects that there is now little popular sentiment in the country favorable to the high protective tariff.

In determining whether natural law has been complied with or violated by the operation of human laws, it is only necessary to carefully estimate the effects of their operation. This may be set down as an infallible guide: if there are injurious effects, natural law has been violated. So, in everything and everywhere, injurious effects prove the violation of natural law.

And then, again, while free trade would make of this country an open market for European goods, it would in turn open to us the markets of Europe by the increased demand for our raw materials for manufacturing purposes. And we would receive larger benefits from free trade than would Europe, in that it would make of the United States a nation of homes. The market prices for products remaining as high or even higher, and the cost of living materially reduced by the removal of the tariff, the profits derived from the sale of our products would make our homes independent and prosperous. Every acre of tillable land would be improved and cultivated, which would more than quadruple the present wealth of the nation. Then the amount of money derived from taxation of increased wealth would be ample to defray the expenses of the government, which would supersede the necessity of the long-talked-of "tariff for revenue only." Naturally this is not a manufacturing, but a producing nation, and with the free circulation of currency and free trade the prosperous owners of its lands could well afford to bear the greater burden of taxation. Then, as now, money would be in the hands of those who reap the largest profits, which under free trade would be the producing classes.

If Europe could furnish her own iron for manufacturing purposes and furnish the manufactured articles to us cheaper than we can get them from home factories, the people would be benefited by the explosion of the various iron and steel trusts; in fact, the inauguration of free trade would put an end to trusts generally. If some legitimate industries had to be abandoned, others would open, promising greater profits. The field of industries would be wide enough for all and would widen with increasing population. Europe would be benefited and the United States would profit immeasurably by free trade.

And why not Europe be benefited from our resources? The earth and the fullness thereof was given in trust to the human race. In the purpose of this splendid gift is the problem of human life. The discovery of what really is the true mission of the race is the solution of this problem. Judging from the selfishness and inhumanity of man in all ages, it would seem that the discovery has never been made. It has been made, however, and the announcement has been before the world for nearly twenty centuries. We now hear it in the call for "the brotherhood of man," sounding from every quarter of the globe. But the majority, blinded by a narrow self-interest, still rush madly on with a feeling of patriotism no broader than the inclosure of national boundary lines. The brotherhood of man, as I understand it, means the broadest patriotism and loyalty—patriotic in the desire to see the human family lifted up to a higher plane of civilization, and loyal to the boundless cause of human liberty. Our religion and our politics should be as broad as civilization. We cannot teach the doctrine of the brotherhood of man, nor exemplify it in our national life, if by our selfishness we violate the spirit of the doctrine. No man can truly believe in this doctrine and favor the protective tariff—a measure that is founded in national selfishness and intolerance. Human laws should be protective after the pattern of nature's first law, which is self-preservation; not protective of greed, but of those who

The brotherhood of man.

need protection from the exactions and ravages of greed.

In our zeal for the consummation of that golden age, the brotherhood of man, let us not lose sight of the pattern given us in nature's first great law. Nor should we overlook the conditions that exist, which clearly define the bounds of the doctrine under discussion. These conditions I will define as the continental boundary lines, with the broad expanse of oceans between, and the color-line. The brotherhood of man does not imply the violent overstepping of these boundary lines. The violation of the first of these conditions consists in unrestricted immigration. The broad Atlantic separates us from the crowded population of the Old World. We are in no way responsible for the laws and institutions of the nations of the Old World, which breed paupers and dangerous classes. We have the right to protect our people from these classes. Nature has provided for such protection in the separation of the two hemispheres by a waste of waters that precludes an easy passage. It is our duty to maintain a perpetual moral, social, and political quarantine against the pestilences of pauperism, heathenism, and lawlessness. Nor should we stop at this. Nationalities of color who would come among us, with peculiar customs, religions, and habits, and persistently refuse to sever their allegiance to pagan laws and institutions and become citizens, should be prohibited by law from landing on our shores. We have the

Restrict immigration.

right and it is our duty to protect our people from the influx of heathens who not only refuse to become citizens, but refuse even to leave buried here the bones of their dead.

Neither does the brotherhood of man imply a violent breaking up of color-lines by amalgamation. These lines are drawn for a purpose unknown to us, but evidently not to be effaced, especially by the unnatural process of amalgamation.

But there should be between nations and peoples a grand unity or brotherhood of interests. Let the gospel be preached to heathens in heathen lands; let the seeds of human liberty be sown and cultivated in every land; but let us be sure that in religious or political missionary work we invite no curse to enter our own land. There is a Christian brotherhood that goes out to the slums and dives of our great cities and persuades the fallen inmates to renounce their lives of shame; but if, unwisely, those moral lepers, unwashed and unclean, were persuaded to enter family circles, the very atmosphere of those homes would be poisoned by the deadly contagion of sin and vice.

So we should refuse to admit to the family circle of this nation the ignorant paupers, the dangerous classes, or hordes of heathens who will not renounce their heathen customs and habits to become citizens. For my own part, I have no patience with impractical and visionary enthusiasts who see in the brotherhood of man the indiscriminate intermingling of all classes, conditions, races, and colors.

There should be a grand international brotherhood of interests, free from jealousies and prejudices. All nations should be governed by a broad international statesmanship, graduated from the school of natural law. Such statesmanship would inaugurate and maintain free international commerce, with open markets and free circulation of currency. Under such a system international trade relations would be reciprocal—the wants of one nation supplied by the surplus (wastes) of another. Some nations are by nature adapted to the supply of resources to other nations smaller and more densely populated. These are adapted to manufacturing. The products of no two nations are alike, owing to difference of climate and soil. By the unobstructed interchange of resources each nation could be supplied with what another produces, which would form a perfect circuit of exchange. And from all these resources manufacturing nations could get their supplies and in turn furnish all with the products of their factories.

Thus the whole national and international machinery of business, trade, and commerce would work in harmony with natural law. And if in harmony with natural law, then no argument is needed to prove that the operation of the system would in every way be conducive of the highest results. This grand system would distribute wealth more equally, and in the place of titled royalty and moneyed aristocracy there would be royalty of character and aristocracy of brains.

GOD IN NATURE

IT may be safely estimated that fully ninety per cent. of all the misery and suffering in the world are due, either directly or indirectly, to violations of natural law, while all the poverty, want, and destitution are due to that cause. Misery and suffering in nearly all cases result from violations of the laws of health, which are a part of natural law. Poverty, want, and destitution are the results of the operation of human institutions of society and government which are founded and perpetuated in violation of natural law. These institutions alone are responsible for "man's inhumanity to man" in all ages. Let these institutions be founded in natural law and there would be an end to poverty, want, and destitution. Aye, more: there would practically be an end to vice and crime. Then let the laws of health be observed by all mankind, and I verily believe the whole world could with one accord look with me "through nature up to nature's God."

Thus the simple obedience to natural law by all mankind would bring to them abundant peace, happiness, and prosperity, and, by removing all the evils which the human family inflicts upon itself, would effectually silence atheism and all unwarranted complaint and scoffing at God's mercy. When man comes to fully realize that by his own inventions and devices, led on by a sordid selfishness, he has heaped upon himself all the evils which scourge and afflict humanity, then will he recognize the great truth of man's free agency. When this truth dawns on his mind the other great truth—that natural laws are instituted for his guidance, and that he is endowed with a moral and intellectual nature by which he may comprehend them, and with a will which should determine his obedience to those laws—will flash resplendent upon his manhood, and he will see that, whereas he was made "a little lower than the angels," he is also capable, by the moral latitude of his free agency, of falling a little lower than the beasts.

If you tell me of inherited diseases of body and mind that are constitutional, for which the victims and sufferers are in no way responsible, I will refer you to the great natural laws of heredity, and call upon you to witness that in all such cases the world over and for all time these laws have been violated. And when I contemplate the manner in which the majority of the human family have lived and continue to live, in open violation of the natural laws of heredity, I wonder that constitutional infirmities of body and mind are not more common and marked than they are. Indeed, when I realize that for all time past and present the human family has obeyed so little and violated so much of natural law in the practical workings of institutions of society and government and of heredity, the wonder to me is that there are any who are physically and mentally sound, and that there are even a few who can be said to be both intellectually and morally great.

To my mind, if there were no evidence of God in nature other than the moral trend of natural law, this evidence alone would be conclusive. But when we couple with this the possibilities of God in man as typified by the life and character of men and women who have risen to grand intellectual and moral heights, rising upward higher and higher and culminating in One who was the physical embodiment of divine attributes, then the evidence of God in nature is sufficient to overwhelm all the deductions of sophistry for all time past and to come.

"Fair are the flowers and the children, but their subtle suggestion is fairer;
Rare is the rose-burst of dawn, but the secret that clasps it is rarer;
Sweet the exultance of song, but the strain that precedes it is sweeter;
And never was poem yet writ, but the meaning outmastered the meter.

"Never a daisy that grows, but a mystery guideth the growing;
Never a river that flows, but a majesty scepters the flowing;
Never a Shakespeare that soared, but a stronger than he did enfold him;
Nor ever a prophet foretells, but a mightier seer hath foretold him.

"Back of the canvas that throbs the thought of the painter
 is thrilling;
Out from the statue that breathes the soul of the sculptor
 is breathing;
Under the joy that is felt lie the infinite issues of feeling;
Crowning the glory revealed is the glory that crowns the re-
 vealing.

"Great are the symbols of being, but that which is symboled
 is greater;
Vast the creation beheld, but vaster the inward creator;
Back of the sound broods the silence, back of the gift stands
 the giving;
Back of the hand that receives thrill the sensitive nerves of
 receiving.

"Space is as nothing to spirit, the deed is outdone by the
 doing;
The heart of the wooer is warm, but warmer the heart of the
 wooing;
And up from the pits where these shiver, and up from the
 heights where those shine,
Twin voices and shadow'd swim starward, and the essence
 of life is divine."

www.ingramcontent.com/pod-product-compliance
Lightning Source LLC
Chambersburg PA
CBHW030402170426
43202CB00010B/1457